Literacy behind Bars

Literacy behind Bars

Successful Reading and Writing Strategies for Use with Incarcerated Youth and Adults

Edited by
Mary E. Styslinger
Karen Gavigan
Kendra S. Albright

ROWMAN & LITTLEFIELD
Lanham • Boulder • New York • London

Published by Rowman & Littlefield
A wholly owned subsidiary of The Rowman & Littlefield Publishing Group, Inc.
4501 Forbes Boulevard, Suite 200, Lanham, Maryland 20706
www.rowman.com

Unit A, Whitacre Mews, 26-34 Stannary Street, London SE11 4AB

Copyright © 2017 by Rowman & Littlefield

British Library Cataloguing in Publication Information Available

Library of Congress Cataloging-in-Publication Data Available

LCCN 2016039818 | ISBN 9781442269255 (pbk. : alk. paper) | ISBN 9781442269262 (electronic)

♾ ™ The paper used in this publication meets the minimum requirements of American National Standard for Information Sciences Permanence of Paper for Printed Library Materials, ANSI/NISO Z39.48-1992.

Printed in the United States of America

Contents

Foreword

William G. Brozo

I have stated many times over the course of my career in speeches, books, and articles (see Brozo, 2011) that our instructional approaches and innovations are only as good as their responsiveness to the neediest adolescents and adults among us. If our literacy strategies and practices are effective for competent and capable adolescents but of little value for struggling readers and writers, then their overall worth must be questioned. Nowhere is this more germane than in the area of corrections education. Because these young men and women failed to receive effective instructional and social supports within schools and communities, they are now at a point in their lives when meaningful and critical literacy interventions may be a necessity for their very survival (Tatum, 2009).

Teachers, social workers, clergy, and other concerned and committed professionals who journey "behind the fences" know well the necessity to learn about these adolescents and adults as individuals. Thus, responsive instruction for incarcerated youth and adults must involve getting to know their learning histories and literacy challenges, as well as their aspirations and interests both inside and outside of the correctional facilities that detain them.

Although we have a large and growing volume of data to delineate the contours of the problem with dropouts and their vulnerabilities to drugs, gangs, and related criminal activity, what is more difficult to find in the professional literature are practical guidelines for leavening the literacy abilities of youth once they find themselves behind bars and fences. To be sure, K–12, school-based preventive approaches that identify and bolster struggling and at-risk readers and writers are far preferred; however, when the system leaves them behind, they cannot be forgotten, as they are in need of responsive literacy work more than at any other time in their lives.

Literacy behind Bars: Successful Reading and Writing Strategies for Use with Incarcerated Youth and Adults is a unique book in that it is devoted entirely to expanding reading and writing literacy for those who have been ill served by traditional schooling policies and practices, which surely contributed to their institutionalization. The authors of the eleven chapters share their stories of rolling up their sleeves and doing the work that must be done to transform the literate lives of imprisoned youth and adults. The lessons learned from these experiences provide instructional direction for anyone who is presently engaged in similar work or is planning to do so. The range of topics taken up by the chapter authors/corrections educators represent important skills and abilities individuals behind bars and fences must develop if they are to leave these institutional settings with an improved chance of success in life outside (Muth, Walker, & Casad, 2014; Vacca, 2004).

Readers of this book will learn how effective practices for increasing word knowledge, improving writing to learn about text and self, fostering critical reading comprehension, and supporting application of literacy strategies across the disciplines were enacted within actual contexts of incarceration. The descriptions of the authors' experiences crafting responsive literacy curriculum and interacting with youth and adults around various reading and writing practices reflect the deep understanding the authors possess of these unique individuals, including an openness to knowing more about who they are within their special institutional circumstances. Thus, one appreciates the authentically contextualized nature of the practices advocated and taught, making it easier to envision the possibilities of similar practices for youth and adults in other correctional settings.

Styslinger, Gavigan, and Albright invite like-minded and similarly dedicated professionals to explore *Literacy behind Bars* in order to become armed with new ideas and insights for enlarging the life potential through literacy of those men and women "behind the fences." For me, each chapter in this book is a reminder that while large data sets may offer shocking evidence of need, the real work of corrections education, as with any interventional work, is most effective when it is local and personal.

REFERENCES

Brozo, W. G. (2011). *RTI and the adolescent reader: Responsive literacy instruction in secondary schools.* New York, NY: Teachers College Press/International Reading Association.

Muth, W. R., Walker, G., & Casad, S. J. (2014). The presence of time in the lived experiences of prisoners: Implications for literacy workers. *Journal of Correctional Education, 65,* 2–11.

Tatum, A. (2009). *Reading for their life: (Re)building the textual lineages of African American adolescent males.* Portsmouth, NH: Heinemann.

Vacca, J. S. (2004). Educated prisoners are less likely to return to prison. *Journal of Correctional Education, 55*(4), 297–305.

Preface

OVERVIEW OF THE FIELD

The United States has the highest prison population rate in the world. Despite the fact that our country has less than 5 percent of the world's population, we house almost 25 percent of the total prison population (Lee, 2015). Over the past forty years, the prison population in the United States has grown from 250,000 to nearly 2.5 million (The Pew Charitable Trusts, 2010), and there has been an especially sharp rise in youth incarceration in the past two decades (Saltman & Gabbard, 2003). These numbers are even more alarming for minority populations (The Pew Charitable Trusts, 2010).

As a nation, the United States incarcerates more citizens than China, Iraq, Iran, Afghanistan, North Korea, Venezuela, and Cuba combined (Hartney, 2006). Our incarceration rate is about six times that of Canada, between six and nine times that of western European countries, and between two and ten times that of northern European countries (Lee, 2015). These numbers are staggering. So what can be done to help stay the ever-increasing numbers?

Studies have shown there is a strong connection between incarceration and education. Hernandez (2011) compared reading scores and graduation results of almost four thousand students and determined that a student who can't read on grade level by third grade is four times less likely to graduate by age nineteen than a child who does read proficiently at that time. If the student who can't read on grade level lives in poverty, then that same student is thirteen times less likely to graduate on time. Couple this fact with a study by researchers at Northeastern University who found that about one in every ten young male high school dropouts is in jail or juvenile detention centers as compared to one in thirty-five young male high school graduates (Sum, Khatiwada, McLaughlin, & Palma, 2009), then the connection between a lack of literacy and the nation's growing prison population can be made. The picture is even bleaker for African Americans, with nearly one in four young black male dropouts incarcerated or otherwise institutionalized on an average day.

There can be no denying the relationship between lack of literacy and the probability of being imprisoned. More than 60 percent of America's inmates are illiterate, and 85 percent of all juvenile offenders have reading problems (Cohen, 2010). But there is some hope, as researchers have indicated a positive correlation between increased literacy and decreased recidivism, particularly if targeted reading interventions are employed. For example, Brunner (1993) has shown that effective reading interventions for juvenile offenders can result in a 20 percent recidivism reduction, not to mention an acquisition of significant reading gains.

As educators, administrators, and community members, we need not only to be aware that we are living in the "age of incarceration" (Hill, 2013), but also recognize the need to develop constructive responses to it. Until this country provides for alternatives to imprisonment, we have a social responsibility to design curriculum and pedagogy that expands literacy instruction in correctional facilities. There are many successful strategies for developing readers and writers while they are incarcerated that can lead to transformation on both sides of the fence. Several of these strategies are shared in the pages of this book.

PURPOSE OF THE BOOK

The authors who contributed to this edited text are committed to making a difference in the literacy lives of those teaching, learning, living, reading, writing, researching, talking, and listening behind the fence. We are professors, teachers, students, librarians, and state department employees. All of us have experience working with incarcerated youth and/or adults. We have written these chapters to serve as a resource for educational and community stakeholders who work with incarcerated youth and adults and for those who work with other at-risk readers and writers.

This book includes examples of authentic literacy practices that have been successfully implemented across a range of prisons and correctional facilities around the nation. Our authors draw upon their experiences working with incarcerated youth and adults in the Southeast, Midwest, Northeast, West Coast, and even the island of Hawaii. The chapters represented here offer an impressive range of stories intermingled with literacy best practices that, whenever possible, include the voices of those who are incarcerated and those who teach and work with them behind the fence.

ORGANIZATION OF THE CHAPTERS

The eleven chapters that follow include a wealth of best practices and accompanying resources that can be implemented with at-risk youth and adults behind and beyond the fence. While we initially resisted organizing the book into sections, specifically one focused around writing and another focused around reading, knowing as we do that the reading and writing processes are intricately interrelated, we found this structure to be simplest. We understand the time constraints of those working in education and want this text to be easily accessed as a helpful resource. So we grouped some chapters in this manner.

This book is divided into three parts. We begin with Part I, "Supporting Writers," as writing is often the "neglected R" (National Commission on Writing, 2003). First, Deborah Appleman shares her experiences and provides guidance in teaching poetry with "Word by Word: Teaching Poetic Economy behind Bars," a chapter filled with the sound and celebration of her students' writing. Next, Timothy R. Bunch shares his story of facilitating a writing workshop with "Teaching to the Heart: Fostering Empathy through Writing Workshop." In "Composing Public Service Announcements: Using Digital Mentor Texts to Support Student Writers in a Juvenile Detention Facility," Kristine E. Pytash provides an overview of a writing project using digital media that encouraged incarcerated youth to investigate and write about important issues. And Kendra S. Albright reveals her experiences developing a graphic novel with incarcerated young men in an effort to help others understand the moral complexity of how young people get involved in gangs in "Writing about the Secrets of Gang Life."

Part II, "Encouraging Readers," begins with a chapter written by Vanessa Irvin. "Call-and-Responsive Reading: Street Literature as Agency for Incarcerated Readers" discusses ways in which teens' "reading" of personal experience serves as an entry point into reading literature that reflects and possibly expands their worldview. Next, "Books behind the Fence," written by Susan McNair, shares the story of a librarian and her efforts to create a friendly, literary-rich hub of learning. Karen Gavigan bridges reading with writing in her chapter, "Creating a Community of Writers Using Graphic Novels," which offers best practices for using graphic novels to engage incarcerated youth in authentic writing engagements. Another chapter that utilizes literature as a springboard, "The Places We Can Go: Book Clubs for Social Justice," written by Jennifer L. Doyle, Elizabeth M. Bemiss, and Mary E. Styslinger, introduces why and how to implement book clubs at a juvenile correctional facility.

Part III, "Inspiring Partnerships," includes stories of successful literacy collaborations across the fence with universities and teachers. This final section begins with "Theme for English B: Teaching and Learning with Incarcerated Youth," written by Peter Williamson, Megan Mercurio, and Constance Walker. This chapter provides a discussion of pedagogical considerations for curricula and strategies that can be effective with incarcerated youth, including an exploration of what new teachers can learn about the promises and pitfalls of practice in these settings. In "Reading Buddies: A School-University Partnership" Mary E. Styslinger and Timothy R. Bunch highlight the benefits of partnerships with novice teachers and share why and how to facilitate a literacy collaboration between incarcerated readers and teacher candidates. And finally, in "Building Bridges across the Disciplines: Professional Development behind the Fence," Victoria A. Oglan and Janie R. Goodman detail a collaborative professional development structure and share their successes and challenges of implementing disciplinary literacy behind the fence.

These sections, chapters, and pages, we hope, will serve as a source of inspiration and encouragement. Much is possible behind bars, especially when we share ideas and work together, knowing as we do that literacy offers the potential for personal and social change.

REFERENCES

Brunner, M. S. (1993). *Reduced recidivism and increased employment opportunity through research-based reading instruction.* Washington, DC: Department of Justice, Office of Juvenile Justice and Delinquency Prevention.

Cohen, S. (2010, December 25). A $5 children's book vs. a $47,000 jail cell: Choose one. *Forbes.* Retrieved from www.forbes.com/sites/stevecohen/2010/12/25/a-5-childrens-book-vs-a-47000-jail-cell-choose-one/#75f435ee76bf

Hartney, C. (2006). *US rates of incarceration: A global perspective.* Research from the National Council on Crime and Delinquency. Retrieved from www.nccdglobal.org/sites/default/files/publication_pdf/factsheet-us-incaaarceration.pdf

Hernandez, D. J. (2011). *Double jeopardy: How third grade reading skills and poverty influence high school graduation.* Retrieved from files.eric.ed.gov/fulltext/ED518818.pdf

Hill, M. L. (2013). Teaching English in the age of incarceration. *English Journal, 102*(4), 16–18.

Lee, M. Y. H. (2015, July 7). Yes the U.S. locks people up at a higher rate than any other country. *Washington Post.* Retrieved from www.washingtonpost.com/news/fact-checker/wp/2015/07/07/yes-u-s-locks-people-up-at-a-higher-rate-than-any-other-country/

National Commission on Writing. (2003). *The neglected "R": The need for a writing revolution.* Retrieved from http://www.collegeboard.com/prod_downloads/writingcom/neglectedr.pdf

The Pew Charitable Trusts. (2010). *Collateral costs: Incarceration's effect on economic mobility.* Washington, DC: The Pew Charitable Trusts. Retrieved from http://pewtrusts.org/~/media/legacy/uploadedfiles/pcs_assets/2010/collateralcosts1pdf.pdf

Saltman, K. J., & Gabbard, D. A. (Eds.). (2003). *Education as enforcement: The militarization and corporatization of schools.* New York, NY: Routledge.

Sum, A., Khatiwada, I., McLaughlin, J., & Palma, S. (2009). *The consequences of dropping out of high school: Joblessness and jailing for high school dropouts and the high cost for taxpayers.* Retrieved from www.northeastern.edu/clms/wp-content/uploads/The_Consequences_of_Dropping_Out_of_High_School.pdf

Acknowledgments

A special thanks to our editor, Charles Harmon; assistant editor, Kathleen O'Brien; and others at Rowman & Littlefield for making this book a reality. We would like to dedicate this book to three groups of important people. First, to our colleagues for their willingness and readiness to share their ideas and experiences behind the fence with others. Next, to the youth and adults with whom we work and about which we write: your attempts to live literacy-rich lives behind bars continue to amaze and inspire us. And last, to our family and friends, without whose support none of this work would be possible: John, Sophie, Anabelle; Frank, John, Matt; Jordan, Brynne, Darcy, and Gordon.

Part I

Supporting Writers

Chapter One

Word by Word

Teaching Poetic Economy behind Bars

Deborah Appleman

"I believe writing can heal the deepest gashes and restore a fragmented soul. My words are all I have and just knowing someone reads them makes me feel alive."—Johnny H., incarcerated writer

On the first day of teaching my very first creative writing class at a high-security prison for men, Terelle rushed up to me during the class break.

"Say," he said. "As long as you are going to be my writing teacher, would you be interested in giving me some feedback on my science fiction novel?"

"Of course," I gushed enthusiastically, eager to please my new students.

"Great! I'll bring it next time. Just so you know, it's 673 pages, single-spaced. It's just that, well, I have so much time to write that I keep adding to it. I've been working on it for the last seven years."

With that, Terelle managed to introduce me to one of the biggest challenges that incarcerated writers face, and one that I didn't expect to find. As do most writing teachers, I have often found that what I need to do most is to encourage recalcitrant writers to get their words on a page, to learn not to pre-edit in their heads, to open the floodgates of their creative imaginations and see what spills out. My free writers are often stingy with their word output; they are tentative and self-censoring. On the other hand, my incarcerated writers often fill their barely bearable days with pages and pages of writing. Much of it is good, some of it is, in fact, brilliant, but nearly all of it needs cutting. Their words, so often stored up for so long, seem to spill out in torrents when they are finally released. Their writing sometimes reminds me of a lush, overgrown flowering plant: the blooms are beautiful and reckless, but the plant has no shape or form. The prospect of trimming is not pleasant, but it's necessary. My incarcerated students do write beautifully, but they overwrite. And I find it difficult to tell them so.

Their tendency to flood each writing opportunity with too many words led me to choose creative writing assignments specifically designed to teach economy and word choice. I settled on three such assignments—the haiku, the sestina, and the six-word memoir. In the pages that follow, I offer a discussion of each assignment and examples from the incarcerated writers.

A WORD ABOUT FORM

First, a word about the constraint of form. In the eight years that I have worked with incarcerated writers, I have realized that writing often represents the only thing that offers them any kind of freedom or liberation. Every single movement, everything they do, is monitored and controlled by others. Such is the nature of incarceration. Their showers are timed; their bathroom breaks are observed; their phone calls are tapped; and their visits with family members are closely watched. The incarcerated men I have taught do know, however, that despite the efforts of the Department of Corrections, their thoughts cannot be controlled nor monitored, and writing offers them an opportunity to express those thoughts freely and without restraints. They find that freedom both remarkable and ironic. As one student said to me, "They tell us when to shit, but you tell us to write anything we want. What are we supposed to do with that?"

So it is with considerable reluctance that I introduce constraints into the only free dimension in their incarcerated lives. Yet, it seems that there are good reasons to do so. Good writers don't simply ignore rules. They learn them and then learn to creatively break them. The constraints offer guardrails, guidelines that help their writing from careening into verbosity. The constraints also help them expand their writing repertoire, familiarizing them with different genres. Interestingly and perhaps not surprisingly, given the life of control and constraint to which they have become habituated, the incarcerated writers seem to accept and even embrace the constraints of form.

HAIKU

We are probably all familiar with haiku as an ancient Japanese art form. The form is frequently taught in secondary schools; the simple three-line form of five syllables, seven syllables, and five syllables offers a simple yet elegant template that offers novice writers a lesson in linguistic economy (see appendix A). As our first exercise in conciseness and constraint, I decided to ask my incarcerated creative writing students to write haiku. I really wasn't sure how this serene and economical form would go over with my verbose writers, but I knew they needed the discipline. I emphasized the fact that it wasn't a childish form but one that inspires reverence and demands control.

Most of the students were familiar with the form, but I reintroduced it, using the handout found in appendix A and going over a few examples together. Then, I passed out colored index cards and asked each student to try to write at least three haiku. The results were amazing. While the assignment forced commonality of form, the content ranged to fit each writer's own purposes for writing. Some focused on death, a common theme in their writing:

Death comes too easy

In too many forms in life

Death has taken me

—Jason MacLennan

Flexible and screaming

Is life

DEATH is stiff nothing

—DOP

Some were beautifully in keeping with haiku's original focus on nature, like these two from Ross:

Camouflage lizard

No one can see you lick

Your own eyeball

Winter's jester

Cold sledding madness

Bitter immersion

And these from Bronson and LaVon:

Dead silence

The woods hold their breath

Waiting for spring

—Bronson

Upon its caress, I awaken

Like a blade of grass

To a beam of sunlight

—LaVon Johnson

For some reason Joe became so taken with the form that he churned out sixty, yes sixty, for his final portfolio. And they are good. Here's just one:

Love is like water

It freezes into ice and

Boils into steam.

And, in the end, we all learned that even seventeen syllables could convey the desolation of incarceration:

Prison is a sad place	My world	A mind is a terrible
Lonely cells in long rows	Is not the one I'm in	Thing to waste, but
Don't go to prison	I exist	Not worse than an entire life
—Terelle Shaw	—Bronson	—Lavon Johnson

THE SESTINA

I gulped hard and held my breath the night I introduced the sestina. What was I thinking, introducing an archaic poetic form, popular in French courts, to an assembly of twenty-first-century men convicted of brutal crimes? I knew they would receive any assignment I gave them with deference and respect, but I really thought that this time I would try their patience.

The sestina is a particular form that focuses on six end words. The end words are the same throughout the lines of the poem, but they appear in a different order in each stanza (see appendix B). Thus, the six words have to be chosen carefully and carry the importance of the poem. I thought this particular exercise would allow my students the space they needed to develop their themes and still emphasize the importance of word choice.

To introduce the sestina, we first read two poems, each titled "Sestina," one by Elizabeth Bishop and one by Dante Alighieri. After we discussed the structure of each poem, I offered the students further explanation of the sestina, written by Ariadne Unst and found in appendix B.

For reasons that I still don't understand, the men really took to the sestina. Perhaps it was the combination of freedom and restriction that enticed them. Not only did they all successfully produce sestinas, but some liked them so well that they kept writing them in what became an improbable kind of prison parlor game. In fact, after one student missed class because his unit was on lockdown, he sent me an apology note written as a sestina!

Below is one of their sestinas. Lu writes to his daughter about the death of his wife, which he caused and she witnessed. Here are his six words:

you, mind, mother, real father, remember, end

And here is the sestina:

Cyann
I can't tell you how much I love you,
You are constantly on my mind,
You look just like your mother,
I wish that I can do more to be a real father,
Cyann, You I will always remember,
Don't worry little girl, this is not the end,

Don't look at it like it's the final end,
Each and everyday I would always think about you,
You are the last thing your mother remembers,
Be strong; don't let people play tricks with your mind,
Wherever you go, always remember that I'm your father,
Always remember that you came from your beloved mother,

Later on in life, you will become a great mother,
Don't worry, I'm still here, it's not the end,
Always remember that you do have a real father,
No one can really tell you what to do, only you,
Your beautiful smile, will always be on my mind,

It's hard to go back, but just try to remember,

Your mom is gone; she will always be remembered,
Always keep in mind, the name of your mother,
Mommy and Daddy are not there, it's not the end,
I hope that you will always have us in mind,
I'm here to answer what questions you have in you,
I always and will always be your father,

Nobody can love you like your mother and father,
I know that what happened, is hard to remember,
I lived my life already and I'm here for you,
Don't forget to go and visit your mother,
Forever always remember to keep us in mind,
This is not our family's final chapter; this is not the end,

You always be on your mother's mind,
When you grow up, don't forget to visit your father,
Your mother and I, our love for you will never end,
You will always be the one we both love and remember,
Life is hard without mom, one day you will be a mother,
Both our lives didn't end; we are kept alive because of you,

Your life is not at an end, keep that in mind,
For you, you now have taken the place of your mother,
Your Father, I will be the last memory of our family to remember

As this example demonstrates, this courtly form of the sestina was an unlikely traveler behind bars, teaching the incarcerated writers the importance of word choice and offering them the power of repetition that the form affords.

THE SIX-WORD MEMOIR

My final example of teaching economy behind bars also revolved around six words, the six-word memoir. The beginnings of this form are now apocryphal. Ernest Hemingway was challenged to write the world's shortest short story, and he bragged that he could do it in six words. The haunting results are now famous:

For Sale. Baby Shoes. Never Worn.

In the last decade or so, six-word memoirs have become a literary fad. Writers, both aspirational and accomplished, have tried their hand at the form, and as a result of a call by *Smith Magazine*, several collections have been published. Here are a few, as quoted in Fershleiser and Smith (2008):

Watching quietly from every door frame.
—Nicole Resseguie

No future, no past. Not lost.
—Matt Brensilver

Catholic school backfired. Sin is in!
—Nikki Beland

Almost a victim of my family.
—Chuck Sangster

I, too, have discovered the suppleness and generalizable usefulness of the genre. I used it in a summer writing program for high school students:

Running from home, never looking back.
Obedience is the burden I bear.

Mothered once, mothered twice, fathered never.
Life doesn't come with stop signs.

In writing workshops with urban students:

I'm walking back in the darkness.

Daddy, don't take away my freedom.

A six-word memoir? Challenge accepted.

I fell, you raised me again.

As a way to respond to literature: tenth graders responding to *Of Mice and Men*:

Livin' off the fatta the land.

Big and small running from trouble.

He can't save himself from softness.

See mice. Pet mice. Kill mice.

Ninth graders responding to *Pericles*:

Love: given and taken from me

I have always been the outcast.

I'm too strong to be broken.

The war against yourself never ends.

And with my college students:

Just look outside. It's all wrong.

But I believe you can fly.

Never underestimate the value of feelings.

Individuality does not equal black sheep.

Humbling hardships, the rose from concrete.

You've had it good. Do something.

Recently, I had the opportunity to sit with a group of accomplished writers that formed a writers' collective in the prison where I teach. These writers meet regularly to share their writing, edit each other's work, and improve their craft. They seized the opportunity to produce six-word memoirs in a recent writers' workshop. Many of their six-word memoirs, like much of their writing, focus on the pain of incarceration:

Six words? For this much pain? —R. B.

Chained by my desire to be free. —W. B.

I'm the penny. Tarnished and worthless. —I. D.

Scorned by all, loved by none. —F. L.

   Some meditate on forgiveness and redemption:

Sunshine captured me, darkness released me. —R. S.

Thorns stay buried in the redeemed —C. C.

   As with all forms, some found the six-word memoir fit their writerly intentions and dispositions. Johnny, who has a short attention span, found them to be a perfect genre for him. He wrote twelve in forty-five minutes; here are three of them:

Why hate, when I can love?

Why die when I can live?

Mom and Dad, I miss you.

   Some of the memoirs offer rays of hope and gratitude:

Your dreams help me succeed further. —I. D.

I've never had support like you. —R. S.

   The writers are currently working on their own six-word memoir collection, one that will include work from many members of the prison population as well as correction officers.

Deborah Appleman

CONCLUSION

In the eight years I have been teaching in prison, I have always been struck by how easily solid and intentional pedagogy travels behind bars. This holds true for the three exercises in poetic economy that I have described in this chapter. We can best help writers, incarcerated or free, by offering them structured forms that help them develop their craft. My incarcerated students don't merely want the freedom to write; they want to learn to write well. It is my fervent hope that these exercises in poetic economy have helped them do just that.

APPENDIX A: HAIKU ASSIGNMENT

Haiku*

If prizes were given to those writers who used the least number of words to communicate the greatest number of thoughts and impressions, poets would be richer than prose writers, and haiku poets would be the richest of all.

One expert on the Japanese haiku called it a "poem recording the essence of a moment keenly perceived in which capture is liked to human nature." Haiku poets write about common, everyday experiences, usually involving natural objects. They avoid complicated words and grammar; many haiku don't have complete sentences. Usually haiku have no metaphors or similes. The most common form of haiku is three short lines, the first and third about the same length and the middle one a bit longer, with no rhyme. But the history of haiku includes many variations.

Some people believe (mistakenly) that a haiku must have seventeen syllables arranged 5/7/5 in lines 1, 2, and 3. The fact is the traditional Japanese haiku poets count "sounds," not syllables. The seventeen sounds of a traditional Japanese haiku take about the same length of time to say as twelve to fifteen English syllables. That's why most North American haiku poets write haiku in three short lines. Each word must help suggest a mood, a scene, or an idea. For this reason, haiku poets usually include words that denote the time of day or time of year, times that carry many associations for all readers.

Here are some famous examples:

Broken and broken   A laughing boy holds out his hands

again on the sea, the moon   until

so easily mends. —Chosu   they are white. —Richard Wright

Among twenty snowy mountains

The only moving thing

Was the eye of the blackbird.—Wallace Stevens

*Portions of this handout are excerpted from *The Teachers & Writers Handbook of Poetic Forms*, Ron Padgett, ed., Teachers & Writers Collaborative, 2000.

APPENDIX B: SESTINA ASSIGNMENT

The Sestina*

Do you have a story to tell? Do you want to tell it in poetry? Then the length and repetition found in the sestina may be the form you need.

The word "sestina" is derived from the Italian *sesto* (sixth). The sestina is a thirty-nine-line form, constructed of six sestets (six-line stanzas) and a final three-line envoi bringing the poem to a close. The words that end each of the lines within the sestet are the same for each of the poem's stanzas, and they repeat in a very particular pattern, as follows:

123456 615243 364125 532614 451362 246531 + envoi (62/14/53)

While this may seem like numerical gibberish at first, there is a very logical pattern, the understanding of which will help you tremendously in constructing a sestina properly. The sestina works very much like a dance, with each stanza representing a reel. Each stanza is based upon the stanza directly preceding it. The order for a stanza peels off the lines of the prior stanza, moving ever inward toward the core: last, first, penultimate, second, antepenultimate, third.

History

Historically, the sestina is a French form. It appeared in France in the twelfth century, initially in the work of Arnaut Daniel. He was one of the troubadours or court poets and singers in the service of French nobles. Troubadours were lyric poets. They began in Provence in the eleventh century. For the next two centuries, they flourished in southern France, eastern Spain, and northern Italy, creating many songs of romantic flirtation and desire. Their name is from the French *trobar*, to "invent or make verse."

Form

In a traditional sestina:

- The lines are grouped into six sestets and a concluding tercet. Thus a Sestina has thirty-nine lines.
- Lines may be of any length. Their length is usually consistent in a single poem.
- The six words that end each of the lines of the first stanza are repeated in a different order at the end of lines in each of the subsequent five stanzas. The particular pattern is given below. This kind of recurrent pattern is "lexical repetition."
- The repeated words are unrhymed.
- The first line of each sestet after the first ends with the same word as the one that ended the last line of the sestet before it.
- In the closing tercet, commonly known as the "envoi," each of the six words are used, with one in the middle of each line and one at the end.
- The pattern of word repetition is as follows, where the words that end the lines of the first sestet are represented by the numbers "1 2 3 4 5 6":

    1 2 3 4 5 6 End words of lines in first sestet.
    6 1 5 2 4 3 End words of lines in second sestet.
    3 6 4 1 2 5 End words of lines in third sestet.
    5 3 2 6 1 4 End words of lines in fourth sestet.
    4 5 1 3 6 2 End words of lines in fifth sestet.
    2 4 6 5 3 1 End words of lines in sixth sestet.
    (6 2) (1 4) (5 3) Middle and end words of lines in tercet

Here are some steps to take in creating a sestina:

1. Decide upon six words that are your candidates for the words that will repeat. I recommend concrete nouns (e.g., wool, chimney, lozenge, floor) and active verbs (e.g., climbs, opens). Alternatively, begin by writing a six-line poem that you want to expand into a sestina. Reorganize that sestet if appropriate to get more interesting end words.
2. On a large blank sheet of paper, write the end words for the first stanza, leaving space to complete the line:

    1
    2
    3

4
5
6

Do the same for the second sestet and so on:

6
1
5
2
4
3

Then for the tercet, write the appropriate two words per line, for example:

6 2

Be sure to follow the above guidelines for form. You will then have written one or two words in each of the thirty-nine lines of the whole poem!

3. Now write the stanzas, using the stepping-stones provided by the chosen words.

4. As with all formal poems nowadays, it is vital that the form does not "drive" your poem. If the rhyme scheme and form begin to feel forced, then the poem's content must be asserted.

5. Traditionally, one keeps the same line length, as that gives the rhythmic repetition that the ear associates with music. It also gives a pleasant appearance on the page. Sometimes a writer wants to vary the line length in order to challenge the listener's or reader's expectations: that is fine if you do it deliberately.

*This handout was created by Ariadne Unst (n.d.) and was condensed and offered in this chapter for instructional purposes. Retrieved from http://www.baymoon.com/~ariadne/form/sestina.htm.

REFERENCES

Fershleiser, R., & Smith, L. (Eds.). (2008). *Not quite what I was planning.* New York, NY: HarperCollins.
Padgett, R. (2000). *The teachers & writers handbook of poetic forms* (2nd ed.). New York, NY: Teachers and Writers Collaborative.
Unst, A. (n.d.). *Poetry form—the sestina.* Retrieved from http://www.baymoon.com/~ariadne/form/sestina.htm

Chapter Two

Teaching to the Heart

Fostering Empathy through Writing Workshop

Timothy R. Bunch

"Could a greater miracle take place than for us to look through each other's eyes for an instant?" (Thoreau, n.d.).

REFLECT PERSONALLY

Young. Naïve. Impassioned. Earnest. Middle class. Unemployed. That was me back in 1990 when I first ventured to teach behind the fence. I had not really considered being from the other side of the fence, as my life experience was largely disconnected from the world most of my students had known, at least in one way or another. I had never had to fear being evicted from our home, or had to worry if I was going to be hungry or uncared for or abandoned, or without electricity, except during an occasional winter storm that was more exciting than dreadful. I had not known a broken or dysfunctional home, had not known suspension or expulsion from school, had not known substance abuse or the consequences of breaking the law.

Oh, and I was white. Though I had grown up in the sixties in the South and had an awareness of racial distinctions and subsequent social issues, I did not learn about white privilege until much later in my life—but I had that, too, it seemed, though early on, I did not know what that really meant, nor did I understand the lens a vast majority of my students might see me through.

Though I had been a victim of intermittent bullying, one crime as a child, and one violent crime as an adult, these were experiences, not my daily existence—experiences that were enough to give me a glimpse into what was often the normal daily existence of many of my students. My experience with heartbreak and disappointment and rejection and loss, normal parts of any life experience, were set against a different canvas. I had been to the beach, seen the mountains, had birthday parties, and built forts in the woods. I had played outside as a kid without fear of being mugged or robbed or shot at. As one of my students glibly commented to me when I was emotionally upset by a fight that had occurred earlier in the day, "Why are you so upset? It's everyday life for us."

Despite the seeming odds, I set out to know my students as people, not mere criminals. My teaching experience came to embody a culture of compassion, drawing on the thin and sometimes fragile line of disparate experience. Though carefully planned and executed, my teaching strategies were characterized by creative risk taking that probed matters of the heart as well as the mind, and promoted academic excellence in quest of life change that might ignite and instill hope. Making text selections and choosing instructional approaches that caught their attention, kept them engaged, and challenged biases were both central and critical. It was through writing workshop that I endeavored to foster empathy, as I, along with my students, learned to reflect personally; connect intentionally; think critically; listen attentively; choose carefully, thoughtfully, and, at times, unwittingly; and celebrate regularly. And it was with this that I made instructional choices that set me on a journey of teaching to the heart.

Through anecdotal reflections, this chapter will present subsections that discuss fostering empathy through writing workshop by reflecting personally; connecting intentionally; thinking critically; listening attentively; choosing carefully; choosing thoughtfully; choosing unwittingly; and celebrating regularly. And by asking yourself over and over, "Could a greater miracle take place than for us to look through each other's eyes for an instant?"

CONNECT INTENTIONALLY

Coined in 1858 by German philosopher Rudolf Lotze, "empathy" finds its origin in art appreciation that depends on the viewer's ability to project his or her personality into the viewed object. The present meaning translates German *einfühlung* as "the psychological identification with or vicarious experiencing of the feelings, thoughts, or attitudes of another" ("Empathy," n.d.). Understanding the concept of empathy, even expressing it myself, was one thing. Teaching it—that was altogether something else, a tall order for a veteran teacher, much less a rookie like myself. Yet, it was empathy, both modeling and teaching it, that became the pulse of my instruction and ultimately came to life in a writing workshop.

Several years into my teaching career, I was introduced to the concept of writing workshop. Not unlike myself, most of my students had little to no experience with this concept; so together we set out on this uncharted territory, gaining inspiration and guidance from Fletcher's *A Writer's Notebook: Unlocking the Writer within You* (1996b) and *Breathing In, Breathing Out: Keeping a Writer's Notebook* (1996a) as well as my own professional experience with a summer writing project.

Writing workshop, a metaphor for collaborative student-centered learning, offered opportunities for students to engage in authentic reading and writing experiences, where reading, writing, thinking, talking, sharing, listening, publishing, and celebrating were normative. I created zones in the classroom—zones for brainstorming, reading, writing, talking, and at times just sitting and daydreaming. I organized times for writing, revising, editing, sharing, and publishing, and I participated along with them, modeling what we came to call the "writerly life" (Heard, 1995).

In time, we were to become a community of writers. But in the early days of this venture, I cannot recount the number of times students informed me quite emphatically that they did not like to read and that they had nothing to write about. I would ask them lots of questions and make suggestions, but their responses were more often than not like Peter Davies in the film *Finding Neverland*: "I still have no idea what to write." I suppose on occasion I may have been clever enough to respond as J. M. Barrie did: "Write about anything. Write about your family; write about the talking whale!" And then, like Peter, one of my students might reply, "What whale?" And I, like Barrie, might reply, "The one that's trapped in your imagination and desperate to get out" ("*Finding Neverland* Quotes," n.d.).

Barrie claimed, "All great writers begin with a good leather binding and a respectable title" ("*Finding Neverland* Quotes," n.d.). So I provided these budding writers with small faux-leather journals to use as their own personal writer's notebooks. Though it is atypical for students to carry books around or to possess pencils outside of class, I was able to get permission for the students to carry their writer's notebooks and to be permitted to secure a pencil when needed. The culture was turning a bit, and it became commonplace to see students not only carrying the writer's notebooks, but storing up their ideas on their pages. I, too, carried mine and wrote along with them and shared my writings as well.

Being clever or witty may certainly have had their place, but I found that knowing my students and selecting text, video clips, and full-length films like *Finding Neverland* (Weinstein, Weissler, & Forster, 1993), *Schindler's List* (Spielberg, Lustig, Molen, & Spielberg, 1993), *Life Is Beautiful* (Gianluigi Braschi, Davis, Ferri, & Benigni, 1998), *The Pianist* (Sarde & Polanski, 2003), *Coach Carter* (Bridgett & Carter, 2005), and *Finding Forrester* (Connery & Van Sant, 2001) that inspired writing was more substantive when it came to teaching to the heart. I showed clips from these, among other films, carefully chosen to spark interest or inspire my students to see the talking whale . . . trapped in their imagination. Reading and writing along with them, I endeavored to evoke authentic writing experiences, but ultimately to probe some memory or imagination in the deepest place in the heart and to help it to get out. It was a risky endeavor to probe their hearts, relive the past, stir up vulnerabilities, and at times unearth very dark places.

THINK CRITICALLY

I am reminded of Forrester's admonition to his young protégé in *Finding Forrester*, "No thinking—that comes later. You must write your first draft with your heart. You rewrite with your head. The first key to writing is . . . to write, not to think!" ("*Finding Forrester* Quotes," n.d.). Though on some level this may be true, thinking and thinking critically was expected. Bloom's taxonomy—the original version (i.e., knowledge, comprehension, application, analysis, synthesis, evaluation), which I later adapted to the newer one (i.e., remembering, understanding, applying, creating, evaluating, analyzing)—was a hallmark of our learning. Students were required to learn the domains and were expected to be able to inform me of the domain they were operating in at any given moment in a lesson or activity. I focused on higher-order thinking processes in reading, writing, listening, and speaking. It was not an option; it was expected and required, as I believed that critical thinking was essential to a quality education and, more importantly for my students, to living a free, responsible life upon parole. Teaching and learning were not just about the academics; they were about lives with names and freckles and varying skin tones and likes and dislikes and hopes and hurts.

LISTEN ATTENTIVELY

Outside my classroom were a parking lot and several enormous trees, with one that canopied the center space. In general it was an unbecoming space with a gravel lot and unkempt earthen beds, but one with much potential both for beauty and instruction. Through a series of grant ventures, my students and I set out to build raised gardens and plant seasonal flowers. It was under that center oak tree and around the small student-designed koi pond that scores of students tilled the soil, planted and pruned and raked, and shared their stories—their heartaches, their fears, their disappointments, and their dreams—often colored by the common thread of hopes that had been unrealized, abandoned, or destroyed.

In "Dream Deferred," Langston Hughes (1990) raised questions that perhaps echoed the silenced voices of my students. Using a cloze poem worksheet, students examined their own dreams deferred, as I examined and modeled my own:

> What happens to my dreams deferred?
> Do they drift off
> like hot air balloons ~
> far away and unseen?
> Do they stand still ~
> lifeless like statues in the park ~
> cold and hard and stony?

It was most important that this classroom of brick and mortar and garden soil be a safe place to disclose, a safe place to grab hold of dreams deferred. Cultivating and nurturing this safe haven was central to my teaching and our mutual learning. Some have described this place, this process, as magical; I describe it as hard work, personal, and relational—an honest place. Self-reflection was crucial, and I came to understand that a prerequisite to empathy is simply paying attention to the person in pain. It was under that oak tree where I really learned to pay attention, to listen.

CHOOSE CAREFULLY

At the heart of creating activities and teaching lessons was making decisions that would make real-world connections between my students and content, particularly text selection. Sharon Draper's *Forged by Fire*

(1998) was a selection that had a profound impact on one of my students, Brandon, who was most predictable when it came to schoolwork.

Right side, back row. Indifferent. Scowling. Sulking. Like a two-year-old sentenced to time-out for more than the bearable three minutes. He appeared to be working on his assignment, but with him, I might not have presumed so optimistically.

I remember that I was writing, periodically glancing up to make sure that everybody was on task. However, lost in my own thoughts and momentarily consumed, I had not noticed that someone was standing near me—waiting—apparently hopeful that I might not have noticed and that he might have been saved by the bell. It was Brandon. I remember our conversation vividly:

"Yes?" I asked as I looked up.

"I finished. Will you read what I wrote?" he asked hesitantly.

"I will listen to *you* read it."

"Mr. Bu—"

"I want to hear *you* read it. No one else will hear. Just me. Go ahead. It's okay. Read it."

I was pretty insistent, and knowing me well, Brandon knew that he did not stand a fighting chance to win a debate on the issue, so he quietly began to read. He held the writing so that we could both see it (see figure 2.1). I followed the lines as he read aloud. And I listened.

When he finished, I asked him to read it again. He looked bewildered, though mostly annoyed.

"I just read it!?" he exclaimed.

"I know, but I want you to read it again."

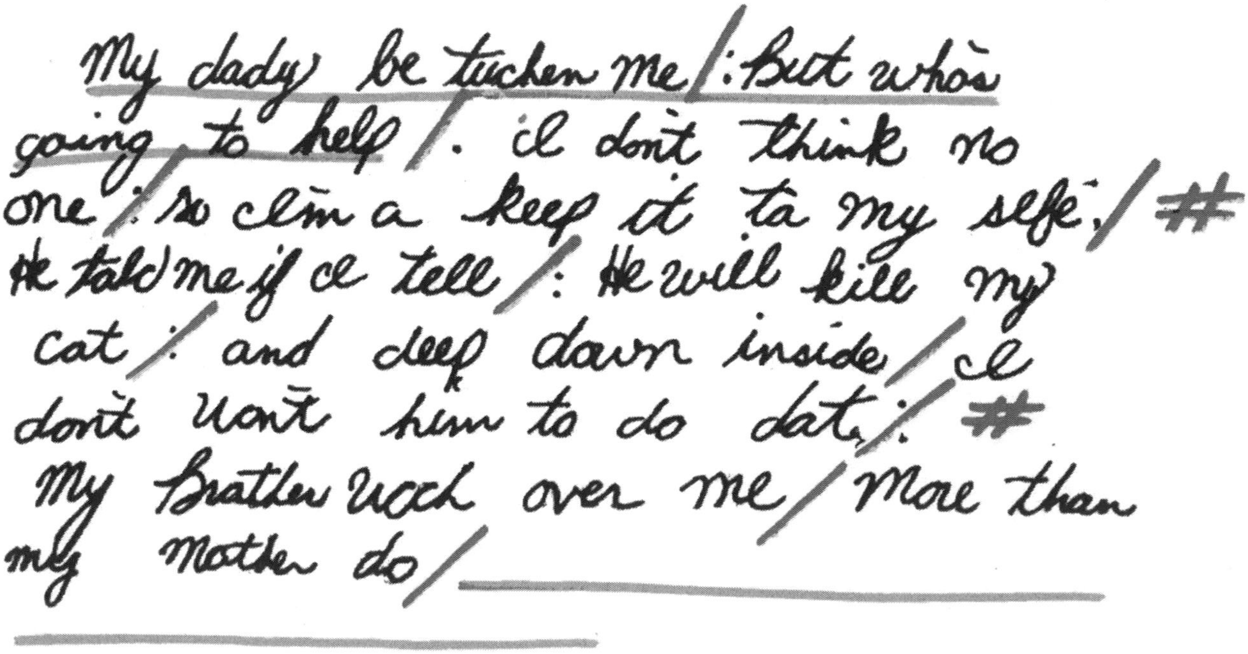

Figure 2.1.   Brandon's original writing. *Brandon Jenkins, student.*

He reluctantly agreed and began to read it again. And again, I listened. Really listened.

"Do you realize what you've written?"

He looked at me—his brow furrowed, letting me know he was frustrated, yet curious.

"You've written a poem."

Brandon stood hovering over me, blankly looking at me and his paper and then back at me. He said nothing.

I asked him to read it again. His look was one of resignation to do whatever I asked. This time, I requested permission to write on his paper as he read. He agreed and began reading it a third time. I marked the lines as he paused and breathed life into those words—*his* words, *his* voice. I instructed him about the marks I had made and asked him to return to his seat and rewrite it. As he returned to his desk, his bewilderment had turned to a subtle, but slightly conspicuous, smile. A few minutes later, he returned to me, poem in hand, with a curious glint in his eye.

"Read it again, Brandon."

"Again? Mr. Bunch," he whined.

"Just read it—for me. I want to hear *you* read it."

He began to read. He had written in his own comfortable African American dialect and when he read aloud, his voice could be heard—loud and clear. It was meaningful and colorful.

I asked if I could hold on to the poem so that I could type it up for him. He smiled, then handed it to me, returned to his seat, gathered his things, and reported to his math class. When I saw Brandon during the next class change, I returned both the original and the typed copy (see figure 2.2) to him.

Later that day, I saw Brandon, who was waiting for his next class to begin. He was holding a piece of paper. This was not so unusual, to have a piece of paper. After all, it was school. But there was something different about the *way* he was holding it—careful, possessive, expectant.

I inquired, "What's that?"

He smiled, looking away. I continued, "What's up with the smile? I've never seen you smile so much. What is it?"

"My poem," he replied. "It's my poem."

I returned a smile and turned toward my office. Something had happened. Something incredible. Something I will never forget. Brandon had finally written something, and it was something he was proud of and treasured. And he wanted me to know.

Brandon later reflected on the text and his poem: "It connects to me personally because I don't like when people hurt little kids. It messes up their minds and hurts them in the long run." Through carefully chosen text and authentic writing experiences, Brandon not only felt empathy but also found the words to express it. When I think about success, I often think of him: he had found his empathetic voice—and his voice had been heard. It had all begun with the selection of a text and had been affirmed by a listening ear.

CHOOSE THOUGHTFULLY

Reflecting on a student's outburst during class, "I never thought about the person I killed," I was reminded of the apparent disconnection between his actions, the impact on others, and the ultimate consequences. One student who had bludgeoned an elderly man nearly to death with a hammer maintained that he had done nothing wrong. Yet another student disputed the injustice he felt because he had been charged with murder rather than involuntary manslaughter after a shooting incident that left his alleged best friend dead.

Helpless
by J. Brandon

My dady be tuch'n me –
            But who's gonna help?
I don't think no one,
So I'm gon' keep it to myse'f.

He tol' me if I tell
He was gon' kill my cat,
An' deep down inside
I don't want him to do dat.

My brotha watch over me –
            More than my mama do.
My dady be tuch'n me –
            But who's gonna help?

Figure 2.2.   Brandon's poem. *Brandon Jenkins, student.*

Paul Fleischman's *Whirligig* (2010) tells the story of a humiliated teenage boy, who, in a failed effort to commit suicide by intentionally wrecking his car, fatally wounds another teen in the crash. Rather than being imprisoned, he is offered forgiveness, which sets him on a journey of responsibility, restitution, and repentance. Integrating artistic expression into the writing workshop, students created original, paper-spiral whirligigs and inscribed original writings about their criminal choices, victim impact, responsibility, restitution, and the hope for forgiveness.

Jonathan, a student in my creative writing class, became a role model among his peers, writing from the heart, then from the mind. He had been separated from his mother in his early childhood and had been estranged into his teen years. His ability to probe his own heart and pen his own experience colored much of his writing that inspired both his peers and me. In a two-voice poem, he wrote of his estranged relationship with his mother and concluded that despite their broken relationship, they shared a common need—the need for each other.

A few months after his writing this poem, some of us who had worked with him stood by as he and his estranged mother were reunited in the quiet, safe haven of my classroom. We may not have walked in his shoes that day, but we walked beside him, seeking to empathize with him, and if not that, to support him. We witnessed hope that day and understood it a bit better as Emily Dickinson wrote: "Hope is the thing with feathers / That perches in the soul / And sings the tune without the words / And never stops / at all" (Franklin, 1999). Though his poetic expression and written confession of sorts did not change Jonathan's experience or resolve his loss, he grew to understand his mother's hard choices that had a profoundly negative impact on him, and ultimately he grew to empathize with her and to forgive.

CHOOSE UNWITTINGLY

"I killed someone."

Six months before hearing those words, I had begun reading *Dawn* (Wiesel, 2006a), the second book in Elie Wiesel's *Night* trilogy (2006b). Wiesel, as most know, was a Nobel Peace Prize winner and Holocaust survivor who chronicled his harrowing experience in the memoir *Night*, a familiar text I had taught before.

The plot of *Dawn* chronicles a few hours in the life of Elisha, a young Holocaust survivor who survived World War II, joined an underground movement, and ultimately wrestled with the value of a human life as he awaited the task of carrying out orders to kill a man who had been kidnapped and held captive.

I, too, wrestled as I considered the dark story line and wondered if, or when, I might use this novel to teach to the heart of my students. So I waited—book read, notes taken, lessons prepared. I waited. Six months passed, and dust had begun to settle. But in the early fall of that year, I rummaged through a slightly dusty file, glanced through, and decided it was time. I did not know quite why, but somehow I knew. It was time. I embarked on the journey, a bit uneasy at the seriousness of the topic and a bit cautious as I could not see around the bend, yet hopeful that this might appeal to the hearts and strike an empathetic cord with at least one of my students.

Only a few pages in, Daven asked to speak with me privately after class. As his classmates left the room, he hung back, slowly gathering his things, seemingly to wait out any onlooker who might be curious to stick around for the conversation. I stood by the door as the last of the students left the room, when he quietly approached me.

"I just wanted to thank you for reading this book," he said, eyes downcast as though there was more that he wanted to say, but dared not.

I replied, "Why is that?"

He said, eyes drifting off slightly, though still downcast, "I think I am like the main character."

"Really?"

"Yeah."

"How so?"

"He lost everything."

Together we recounted the things the main character had lost: "an orphan bereft not only of father and mother, but of hope . . . blighted childhood . . . open wounds . . . native town occupied . . . his home in foreign hands" (Wiesel, 2006, p. vii). He shared how he could relate as he felt that he had lost everything: his home, his parents, his freedom.

Although I could see some relation, and although I was glad to see him making personal connections, I was still a bit puzzled. There seemed to be more that he was *relating to*. To my further probing, he inquired, "You know why I'm here, right?"

I looked at him, silent. I considered that confessing that I did not know might imply that I did not care. I considered that any feeble excuses might fall short of what he expected. Seconds, which seemed like minutes, passed, and I finally confessed, "No, I am sorry, but I don't."

Solemnly, he looked up, the glint of desperation and hopelessness in his eye. "I killed someone."

Those words still reverberate in my mind, a clashing cymbal, harsh and dissonant. In that fleeting moment, my soul reached up, earnestly appealing to God to give me wisdom as I attempted to respond to this young man of seventeen, whose desperate and apparently hopeless confession begged my response.

"I think there is one distinct difference between you and Elisha. Unlike him, you have hope. The very fact that we are having this conversation tells me that there is hope, for you, Daven. There is hope."

In the days that followed, we had several other conversations. In the weeks that followed, we finished the novel. In the months that followed, Daven embraced the tedious challenge of facing responsibility for his crime—and ultimately facing his victim's mother, who courageously forgave him. In the years that followed, Daven was released on parole and, from what I last heard, has a job and has become a productive citizen.

In *On the Pulse of Morning*, Maya Angelou (1993) penned, "History, despite its wrenching pain, cannot be unlived, but if faced with courage, need not be lived again." Daven faced his history and moved on. And it all began with an instructional decision—though unwitting—to appeal to the individual needs of the students in my care, a decision to teach to the heart, a decision to inspire hope in the life of a child, who in his eyes had lost everything.

CELEBRATE REGULARLY

I did not teach arithmetic, but it was important that what I did teach *added up* in the whole scheme of my students' lives. I recall vividly, as one of my students put it, "I felt like a little star," as he shared how he felt about his writing and perspectives being considered, valued, and celebrated. As I paused to listen to hear their voices, to understand their viewpoints, to challenge my own blighted perspectives, I gained insights that did not enable their often justified and understandable but ill-conceived and self-entitled views about life or the law, but helped me to learn to empathize with them, and celebrate with them as they transcended dark places to come out on the other side, hopeful. Believing that worldviews are developed through nature, nurture, and personal choice, I set out to know my students, to live life with them, to expose them to other viewpoints through reading and writing in response to carefully chosen texts that spoke to the heart of issues that they could relate to, and to inspire hope in their often fragmented lives.

Pursuing vigilance and tenacity, embracing vulnerability, and establishing high expectations—while also setting and maintaining boundaries—are foundational prerequisites to foster empathy. So what are the requirements for those who teach to the heart to foster it? Reflect personally. Connect intentionally. Think critically. Listen attentively. Choose carefully, thoughtfully and, at times, unwittingly. But choose. And finally, celebrate regularly as you "look through each other's eyes for an instant" (Thoreau, n.d.).

REFERENCES

Angelou, M. (1993). *On the pulse of morning.* New York, NY: Random House. Retrieved from http://www.brainyquote.com/quotes/ quotes/m/mayaangelo387255.html

Bridgett, S. (Producer), & Carter, T. (Director). (2005). *Coach Carter* [DVD]. United States: Paramount.

Connery, S. (Producer), & Van Sant, G. (Director). (2001). *Finding Forrester* [DVD]. United States: Columbia Pictures.

Draper, S. (1998). *Forged by fire.* New York, NY: Simon Pulse—Simon & Schuster.

Empathy. (n.d.). In *Online Etymology Dictionary.* Retrieved from http://dictionary.reference.com/browse/empathy

Finding Forrester quotes. (n.d.). Retrieved from http://www.imdb.com/title/tt0181536/quotes

Finding Neverland quotes. (n.d.). Retrieved from http://www.imdb.com/title/tt0308644/quotes

Fleischman, P. (2010). *Whirligig.* New York, NY: Square Fish.

Fletcher, R. (1996a). *Breathing in, breathing out: Keeping a writer's notebook.* Portsmouth, NH: Heinemann.

Fletcher, R. (1996b). *A writer's notebook: Unlocking the writer within you.* New York, NY: Harper Trophy.

Franklin, R. W. (Ed.). (1999). *The poems of Emily Dickinson.* Cambridge, MA: Harvard University Press.

Gianluigi Braschi, G., Davis, J., Ferri, E. (Producers), & Benigni, R. (Director). (1998). *Life is beautiful* [DVD]. United States: Miramax.

Heard, G. (1995). *Writing toward home: Tales and lessons to find your way.* Portsmouth, NH: Heinemann.

Hughes, L. (1990). *Selected poems of Langston Hughes.* New York, NY: Random House.

Sarde, A. (Producer), & Polanski, R. (Director). (2003). *The pianist* [DVD]. France, Germany, Russia: R. P. Productions.

Spielberg, S., Lustig, B., Molen, G. R. (Producers), & Spielberg, S. (Director). (1993). *Schindler's list* [DVD]. United States: Universal Pictures, Amblin Entertainment.

Thoreau, H. D. (n.d.). In Brainyquote online. Retrieved from http://www.brainyquote.com/quotes/quotes/d/danielgole585881.html

Weinstein, H., Weissler, B. (Producers), & Forster, M. (Director). (1993). *Finding Neverland* [DVD]. United States: Miramax.

Wiesel, E. (2006a). *Dawn.* New York, NY: Hill & Wang, a division of Farrar, Straus and Giroux. (Original work published 1961.)

Wiesel, E. (2006b). *Night* trilogy (M. Wiesel, Trans.). New York, NY: Hill & Wang, a division of Farrar, Straus and Giroux.

Chapter Three

Composing Public Service Announcements

Using Digital Mentor Texts to Support Student Writers in a Juvenile Detention Facility

Kristine E. Pytash

"Of all our cognitive capacities, imagination is the one that permits us to give credence to alternative realities. It allows us to break with the taken for granted, to set aside familiar distinctions and definitions" (Greene, 1995, p. 3).

Sean and Jerome were two students I met during the summer of 2014 at a county juvenile detention facility, a short-term pre-adjudication and post-adjudication correctional facility. I had been facilitating a writing workshop in this county for over a year and decided to engage youth in a larger writing project spanning multiple weeks (Pytash, 2016). Sean and Jerome were part of a cognitive behavioral therapy (CBT) group designed to provide additional intense interventions to repeat offenders. They each were sixteen years old and self-identified as African American. Sean attended a virtual online school and Jerome attended a local high school.

The goal of the project was to provide youth an opportunity to compose print and digital text around a topic they felt was important in their lives and in their communities. Youth researched their topic and composed in a variety of genres to better understand the topic, to voice their experiences, and to explore its importance. Sean decided to investigate the topic of peer pressure, as he believed it was something he had succumbed to in his life. Jerome investigated the importance of music in his community, as music was something he was passionate about and believed was important to many adolescents' lives.

The goal of the writing instruction was to develop students' writing abilities; however, it was also designed for the writing to be authentic and relevant to youths' lives. One way this happened was by allowing students to write about topics important in their lives and communities. In addition, instructional approaches provided youth opportunities to view writing as a powerful tool used to voice lived experiences, amplify beliefs, and convey ideas. The goal of this chapter is to provide insight into instruction that invites youth in juvenile detention centers to learn more about the writing process and to voice their lived experiences through writing.

SUPPORTING WRITERS

One instructional approach for the teaching of writing is the study of mentor texts. Mentor texts are exemplary pieces of writing that students can analyze to learn about a particular genre. The goal is to provide students with models of writing they can emulate when writing original pieces. Students are provided a "vision" for their writing by gaining knowledge about how a piece might be written (Ray, 2006). Smith (1983) coined the phrase "reading like writers" to explain this process. With teacher guidance, students are immersed in the study of a particular genre. Active close reading and analyzing draws students' attention to particular features of the genre. Specifically, students begin to notice the purpose, audience, form, and structure of the genre. This provides opportunities for students to consider what makes a piece of writing excellent within a particular genre. It also helps students ask questions about and consider the intentional decisions authors make while crafting a piece of writing. Students benefit from this close study of genre as it assists them when they write an original piece.

Composing Digital Texts

Studying mentor texts to support writers is an instructional approach that has been documented widely when writing print-based genres (Gallagher, 2011; Ray, 2006) and more recently has been used to support students when crafting digital texts (Hicks, 2013). Hicks (2013) advocates that when studying digital writing, students must analyze the modes, media, audience, purpose of the composition, and the situation. It is important for students to recognize how these elements of digital writing work together to convey meaning. For example, it would be important when analyzing video composition for students to focus on how the images and audio work together, in addition to considering the purpose of the video composition and the intended viewing audience.

Similar to studying writing that is print based, using a digital text as a mentor text provides students insight into the composition process. This in turn assists students' thinking when they are composing. By first analyzing the "intentional choices about craft," students can engage in the creative work of writing digitally (Hicks, 2013, p. 19). Because they have already considered why an author would choose to use specific video or images along with a particular style of music or audio, students are prepared to make choices about the media elements they should use and why. In addition, the unexpected benefit of teaching students to deconstruct and analyze media as part of the writing process is that not only do students learn to compose and produce texts, but they become critical consumers of digital media.

Digital Writing Instruction at the Detention Center

The goal of the writing instruction was to provide youth opportunities to write about topics grounded in their lives so that they might be invested in their writing and also so they could experience how writing can be a powerful way to articulate beliefs, opinions, and lived experiences. In addition, it was an important goal for youth to compose with digital tools so they could reflect on how their ideas could be conveyed through written words, images, and sound.

During the second week of our project, youth studied and composed public service announcements (PSAs). PSAs are persuasive messages directed to the public or a specific community. They are used to inform and persuade the audience to take action by advocating for a particular position or stance. For example, famous PSAs include Smokey the Bear and the Partnership for a Drug Free America's "This is your brain on drugs" ad campaign.

Max, a preservice teacher in my program, and I cotaught the writing unit. We began the unit by explaining that PSAs are typically informative, in that specific information is used to convey knowledge (e.g., using statistics); however, we also explained that the goals of PSAs are to persuade people to think about a particular topic in a certain way. We decided to use mentor PSAs that focused on texting while driving, since we thought this topic might be relevant to their lives.

The gradual release model (Pearson & Gallagher, 1983) was used to engage students in a series of close watching of PSAs. The gradual release model is an instructional approach that begins with the teacher providing scaffolds and gradually moves students to more independent learning. My first step was to make sure students had background knowledge of what a PSA is by showing them the Toyota PSA (Shadow99, 2012). My second step was to conduct a think-aloud while rewatching the Toyota PSA. During this time, I told students what I noticed about how the PSA was composed. I shared that I immediately noticed the piano music playing in the background and that the tone was ominous. I pointed out the PSA begins with a series of incidents in which the adolescent boy is clumsy doing routine tasks (e.g., eating cereal or walking down the street) and ends with the boy texting while driving and getting into a car accident. I also pointed out that the first half of the video is in black and white. I then talked about how at the halfway point the video changes. Color video is used to show the boy engaged in all the same tasks, but not texting and therefore acting responsibly. I also pointed out that the music shifted to a happier tone and that throughout the entire PSA there is no language spoken. I wrote these ideas on a sheet of chart paper and called this our *list of noticings*. My goal was to actively guide students' attention to particular details of the PSA. In particular, I wanted students to notice how the author used multiple modes to convey a specific message and persuade the audience not to text when driving.

The next step of instruction was to provide students the opportunity to deconstruct a PSA with a peer. Students watched a different PSA about texting and driving (Gentry, 2014) and then with their peer talked about what features they noticed. We added their responses to the initial list of noticings. Finally, we wanted students to have an opportunity to work independently. To guide their thinking, we provided youth with the following questions:

1. What is the focus or main message that the author is trying to convey?
2. Who is the intended audience? Why do you think this?
3. What does the author want the audience to think? How do you know this?
4. What specific information is being used? For example, does the author use statistics?
5. What visuals are used? Is this a video, or are still images used?
6. Is audio used? If so, what is the audio (e.g., music or spoken word)?
7. Are visuals and audio used at the same time?

After watching a PSA, youth independently answered these questions. After they completed the questions, we talked as a group about what they noticed. Again, we added their ideas to our list of noticings. This list was posted in the classroom so youth could refer to the list when they were creating their PSAs. The goal of this instruction was to draw students' attention to the particular features we noticed about PSAs so they had the opportunity to draw on this knowledge when composing their original PSAs.

SEAN AND JEROME'S PUBLIC SERVICE ANNOUNCEMENTS

During this composition process, both Jerome and Sean focused primarily on the visual element and how their images would convey certain ideas. Sean began his piece with the words "Peer Pressure" written on the screen and the sounds of sirens in the background. For the rest of his PSA, he alternated slides of words with slides of images, words, and sounds. For example, he included a slide with an image of an adolescent reaching for a cigarette from another adolescent, and he wrote the words "Take one, Come on, try it" over the picture. The next frame used the text "peer pressure can be bad," to emphasize the meaning from the images. Sean followed this with an image of a boy in a classroom with his hands over his head. Sean wrote the words "I'm so confused" on the top of the picture and included a sound effect of a noisy room. The noise added a layer to the image and words, giving the viewer a sense of being overwhelmed. He explained, "Like there is peer pressure that can happen in the classroom. A lot of people don't think about it, but peer pressure happens a lot in school."

Sean continued to play with the combination of words, images, and sound by including a slide stating that peer pressure normally involves violence and then an image of a gun with the words "pull the trigger." He later explained, "People also use peer pressure when they don't want to do the dirty work and want other people to do it for them." In addition, he included a slide of adolescents fighting and the words "fight, fight, fight," in the background. He explained, "People will provoke fights just for something to watch—so people use peer pressure for amusement, too." His final slide read, "Peer pressure has its ups and downs, but it is up to you to overcome peer pressure." Sean explained, "This was really just information and what I learned about peer pressure. But then I used my experiences to pick the pictures and put it all together."

Similar to Sean, Jerome created his PSA to include multiple modes to convey his ideas. Jerome opened his piece with an image of earphones and the word "Listen." He then showed a piano with the words "fall in tune," and then a recording studio with the words "feel the beat." Jerome was trying to match the words he selected (like "fall in tune") with the image he selected (i.e., a piano). He explained that he paid careful attention to the images as they "represent music." He then intentionally decided to include pictures of people—one of a boy playing the guitar, another of people hand in hand. He wanted the view to consider how music can "bring people together." Similar to Sean, Jerome added sound to his public service announcement; however, instead of multiple sound effects, he used a song by Drake, "Lord Knows," because he felt the lyrics captured the essence of what music does for people. He explained:

> I used Drake's song in the background because he sings, "they take the greats from the past and compare us." He [Drake] is talking about music, and he is saying that who you are is ok. I felt like that song had powerful lyrics, and my whole video is on the power of music.

For Jerome, the combination of the Drake lyrics with his images and words created an exploration of the power of music.

Sean and Jerome began to consider how the combination of text, images, and sound contributed to the overall message they wanted to convey. They also engaged in playfully trying a combination of text, images, and sound until they found the best grouping. For Sean, each slide represented peer pressure as "good" or "bad" and, therefore, on each slide the text, images, and sound conveyed that particular message. For Jerome, the overall composition was to convince people that music is inspirational in lives.

FINAL THOUGHTS

As new technologies and digital media influence the writing process and our conceptions of writing, it is important for youth to have opportunities to compose with digital tools. By examining PSAs, youth had the opportunity to think strategically about how to craft a persuasive message about a topic they felt was important. In addition, by deconstructing the mentor texts, youth had opportunities to learn how authors craft persuasive messages using a variety of modes (e.g., images, audio, video).

Wilson (2004) argues, "We must resist the temptation to think about literacy as though it were, indeed, just one thing. . . . To deny the extent to which people engage with various forms of literacy-related activity and practice is to deny a sense of heterogeneity and difference" (p. 87). When we broaden our notions of what it means to engage in literacy and consider the various forms and semiotic systems, we can recognize the very complex and meaningful literacy practices with which we can engage youth. Engagement in both traditional print and multimodal writing allowed these students to focus on life experiences and find opportunities to express who they are, what they believe, and how they want to represent themselves and issues.

Digital writing allows students to develop their ideas by using a variety of meaning-making modes. Sean and Jerome described being most engaged when creating their PSAs because they were motivated by using images and sound to convey their ideas. This was a new way to experience composing, one they did not have in their traditional school settings. When engaged in composing their PSAs, Sean and Jerome were engaged in sophisticated design choices as they produced compositions composed of multiple modes, requiring them to consider the purpose of the genre. They viewed the combination of images, text, and sound as important in conveying their messages. This provided them the opportunity to consider how the collection of modes contributed to the overall meaning of the piece and its intended effect on the audience. Their choices were deliberate and important in the overall message they were intending to convey.

REFERENCES

Gallagher, K. (2011). *Write like this: Teaching real-world writing through modeling and mentor texts*. Portland, ME: Stenhouse.
Gentry, T. (2014, August 11). *Don't text and drive PSA* [Video file]. Retrieved from https://www.youtube.com/watch?v=rClJW9gnchc
Greene, M. (1995). *Releasing the imagination: Essays on education, the arts, and social change*. San Francisco, CA: Jossey-Bass.
Hicks, T. (2013). *Crafting digital writing*. Portsmouth, NH: Heinemann.
Pearson, P. D., & Gallagher, M. C. (1983). The instruction of reading comprehension. *Contemporary Educational Psychology, 8*(3), 317–344.
Pytash, K. E. (2016). Composing screenplays: Youth in detention centers as creative meaning-makers. *English Journal, 105*(5), 53–60.
Ray, K. W. (2006). *Study driven: A framework for planning units of study in the writing workshop*. Portsmouth, NH: Heinemann.
Shadow99. (2012, February 13). *Toyota teen drive PSA—Texting while driving* [Video file]. Retrieved from https://www.youtube.com/watch?v=nivWUpq6j9g
Smith, F. (1983). Reading like a writer. *Language Arts, 60*(5), 558–567.

Wilson, A. (2004). Four days and a breakfast: Time, space, and literacy/ies in the prison community. In K. Leander & Margaret Sheehy (Eds.), *Spatializing literacy research and practice* (pp. 67–90). New York, NY: Peter Lang.

Chapter Four

Writing about the Secrets of Gang Life

Kendra S. Albright

"This is a war and the gang members are winning" (Gamez as cited in Weissert, 2005).

This chapter reveals the experiences of developing a graphic novel with incarcerated young men, to help other young adults understand the moral complexity of how young people get involved in gangs. Conducted over a period of four weeks, youth at a Department of Juvenile Justice high school drafted the story of a young man who loses his mother to AIDS and is forced to move with his younger sister to another city to live with relatives. In order to make friends and fit in with his new family and friends, the young man makes choices that get him into serious trouble after joining a local youth gang. This chapter explains the process of writing a graphic novel with incarcerated youth and its impact on the writers themselves.

BACKGROUND OF THE PROJECT

According to the Federal Bureau of Investigation (FBI, n.d.), there are approximately thirty-three thousand street, motorcycle, and prison gangs in the United States with about 1.4 million members. Many of these gangs are well organized and use violence to support their illegal generation of monies through robbery, drug and gun trafficking, fraud and extortion, and prostitution. Gangs account for an average of 48 percent of violent crime in most jurisdictions, and up to 90 percent in others (National Gang Intelligence Center, 2011). According to James Howell of the National Gang Center, "In the past five years we've seen an 8 percent increase in number of gangs, an 11 percent increase in members and a 23 percent increase in gang-related homicides" (Axelrod, 2015).

While these estimates are provided by the FBI, the bureau does not guarantee the accuracy of the statistics. Data is difficult to collect on gangs and is dependent upon the reports from a range of agencies, including the National Drug Intelligence Center, the Bureau of Prisons, state correctional facilities, and local law enforcement agencies, in addition to the National Gang Intelligence Center. Estimates, therefore, may be somewhat different than in actual practice. What is clear, however, is the scope and severity of the problems associated with gang activities.

While gangs have been primarily associated with larger cities, about 40 percent of suburban counties and smaller cities saw the emergence of gang activity in the 1990s (National Gang Center, 2012). Of great concern is the number of young people joining gangs. While there is no standard or agreed-upon definition of "gang" across law enforcement agencies, the National Youth Gang Survey defines a gang as "a group of youths or young adults" within a law enforcement jurisdiction that those agencies or communities are "willing to identify as a 'gang'" (National Gang Center, 2012). The definition of youth gangs typically excludes motorcycle gangs, hate or ideology groups, prison gangs, and exclusively adult gangs. More than three out of five gang members are adults, however, and the majority are male. Despite this ratio, gangs are now recruiting in public schools and targeting children as young as nine because the judicial system is more lenient on younger children and first-time offenders. This puts the younger members at risk since they can take on riskier jobs for the gang (National Crime Prevention Council, 2016).

Two factors are most associated with gang violence: drug-related factors and intergang violence (National Gang Center, 2012). Gangs often mark their territory and require their members to show affiliation through wearing certain colors, symbols, or tattoos. They may mark and destroy property as a way of demonstrating their turf boundaries to rival gangs. When a member of one gang enters the territory of another, violence often erupts.

Prevention programs across the United States are now targeting middle schoolers to curb the increasing gang membership among America's youth. One way to reach adolescents and young adults is through the use of graphic novels. Graphic novels have been demonstrated to increase motivation and interest in young adults (Gavigan, 2012; Short, Randolph-Seng, & McKenny, 2013). The engaging format of graphic novels facilitates reading and increases the retention of information in young adults (Gavigan, 2012). The structure of the story encourages the reader to become invested in learning as the story unfolds in an authentic, realistic manner. "The graphic novel goes beyond the cognitive aspects activated by traditional textbooks to engage students on an emotional level as well" (Short et al., 2013, p. 297). There is increasing evidence that graphic novels may contribute to learning for students with various learning styles and capabilities (Botzakis, 2009; Carter, 2007; Gavigan, 2012; Monnin, 2008). In sum, graphic novels can be an important way to inspire incarcerated youth to consider the consequences of joining a gang.

PROCESS

The overall objective of this project was for incarcerated youth to write an age- and culturally appropriate graphic novel about gangs that would serve as a tool for preventing youth from joining gangs. Beginning in the fall, two researchers from a local state university met once a week with two classes of young incarcerated men, ages fifteen to seventeen, from a state-affiliated Department of Juvenile Justice (DJJ) high school. The researchers had previously worked with the DJJ on a similar project, developing a story about HIV/AIDS prevention for teens. The project was highly successful in its ability to convey accurate and factual knowledge to teens in a format that was highly accessible and interesting to the target population. Titled *AIDS in the End Zone (AIEZ)*, the graphic novel was published in 2014 (Albright & Gavigan, 2014). The researchers planned to replicate the process used in the development of *AIEZ* on a different topic and compare results with the previous study.

The first meeting consisted of introductions and an overview of the process. DJJ students were shown different types of graphic novel genres, including superheroes, manga, and a copy of *AIEZ*. After some discussion, the students in each class immediately launched into the process and decided they wanted to build on one of the characters in *AIEZ*, a shadowy, loner character named Seth, who befriends the main character in *AIEZ*, convincing him of the importance to get tested for HIV. In *AIEZ*, Seth's mother has AIDS and his younger sister is HIV positive.

STORY LINE DEVELOPMENT

In this new graphic novel about gangs, the students decided that Seth's mother, Karen, who is Puerto Rican, has recently died of complications from AIDS. Karen had always been a positive influence on Seth and his sister, and held the family together after Seth's father, an African American gangster, died in prison. He was incarcerated after he shot and killed someone while dealing drugs to make money to support his family.

After the death of his mother, Seth and his sister move from South Carolina to Atlanta to live with their cousin's family. Once they arrive in Atlanta, Seth's cousin, "Loco," invites Seth to join a gang called the "NAPA (Nobody Ain't Perfect Always) Boys." After being pressured by Loco and his friends, Seth agrees and assumes his gang name of "Spook." Not long after joining the NAPA Boys, Seth begins to follow in his father's footsteps, selling drugs (see figure 4.1) and stealing to make money to help support his sister, whom he has always looked after. Spook also spends the money he makes to support his Hispanic girlfriend, Simone Cortez, so she can go to college. She loves Spook, and he is good to her because he loves her, too.

Spook and Loco are arrested for dealing drugs and stealing, and they are sent to the DJJ for two years. When they get out, they want to get their lives straight. They start working at fast food restaurants, waiting for their probation to end so they can join the Marines. Meanwhile, Duke is in jail and wants Spook to kill Officer Pedro. But Spook and Loco both refuse because they're trying to stay out of jail. Instead, Quay kills Officer Pedro, whose murder is investigated by Detective Michael Johnson. C-Loc kills Duke when Duke gets out of jail. C-Loc is sympathetic to Spook and Loco for wanting to get out and start a better life. So C-Loc gives money to Spook and Loco to help them. But LB would not understand why C-Loc would help Spook and Loco, so C-Loc can never tell anybody he gave them any help. C-Loc is a good guy but a killer.

It was surprising how quickly the students drafted the plot and developed characters (see appendix A) on the first day. There were, however, many opinions and disagreements about the details of the story, which was an important part of the process. First, the different opinions helped the group make collective decisions and come to consensus. Second, while some of the individual opinions might have been morally questionable, collective decisions guided the group into making sound decisions that demonstrated both an understanding of the problems faced by the gang members and their judgment of right and wrong and acceptance of appropriate consequences. Third, the students at DJJ were not only divided on their opinions, but they were physically divided in the classroom, into what appeared to be their own gang membership. While this was not verbally confirmed, it was implicit in their interactions within and between the groups. In addition to their story development, they would talk about gang colors, signs, and tattoos (e.g., spiderwebs and teardrops). For example, they explained that a tattoo with a spiderweb reflects potential homicides committed, where each spider in the web represents a person he (the person with the tattoo) has killed. Another gang tattoo that might represent killing someone is the teardrop tattoo. According to the CorrectionsOne (2014) website, "In some places, the tattoo can mean a lengthy prison sentence, while in others it signifies that the wearer has committed murder." The same website also reports that the spiderweb tattoo typically represents a lengthy prison term.

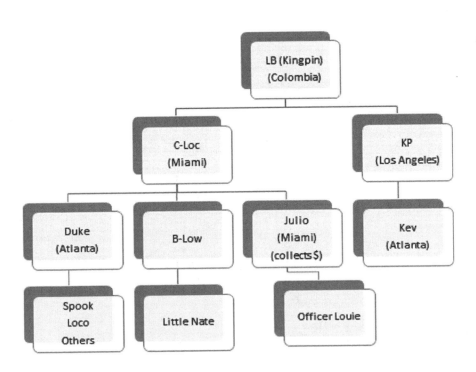

Figure 4.1.   Drug cartel chart in the story. *Kendra Albright, chapter author.*

BLOCKING THE SCENES

Once the students completed the final draft of the story, the next step was to block the scenes. The purpose of this exercise is to help translate the story into a storyboard that can be used to develop the actual illustrations. In this story, the students created twenty-four scenes from which the illustrations would be developed (see appendix B). While the total number of scenes is twenty-four, there may be more than twenty-four illustrations to convey all of the scenes as some may require more than one panel.

In addition to the story itself, the students also wanted to include supporting material similar to that found in *AIDS in the End Zone*. They wanted to include a glossary of terms. This was a particularly interesting idea because of the vernacular used in gang language as well as current language used by young people in general (see table 4.1).

The students also wanted to include a section on interesting facts called "Did You Know?" at the end of the novel. Suggested topics included:

- How many people are killed by gang violence
- How many people are injured by gang violence
- How many people are jailed for gang violence
- How many teens are rejailed (rate of recidivism)
- How many gang members do not have parents
- How many innocent bystanders are hurt or killed by gang violence
- How much money drug dealers actually make
- Reasons why people join gangs
- Statistics about MS-13—illegal immigrants coming into Texas; the Red Cross gives them cell phones so they can communicate with their families, but instead, MS-13 is using these phones to connect with young men to get them into gangs (some of the DJJ students had joined gangs and reported that MS-13 is involved in infiltrating facilities such as theirs).
- Names of gangs:

  - Crips (blue)
  - Bloods (red)
  - Latin Kings (black and gold)
  - Vicelords (yellow and purple)
  - Folks (yellow and black)
  - MS-13 (red)

Table 4.1.   Terms and their meanings.

Term	Meaning
Bagged	Arrested
Pipe	Gun
OP	Other people; opponent Example: "Let's go ride on this OP [other people or other people's things]—get him/kill him [OP]" (means like "opponent"—for rival gang members)
Thrax	Something good Example: "Them shoes is thrax"
Drack	How you live Example: If asking for a dollar that is owed, "Get it like drack." (Like Dracula—beat me up for this.)
Lev	Cool
Lame	Not cool

- The difference between a neighborhood gang and a street gang
- Dropout rate for gang members
- Bullying by gangs
- Pressure from other family members to join a gang if you're brought up in a gang family

The students also wanted to include sidebars throughout the illustrated pages, supporting the content of the story with factual information. Some suggested topics for the sidebars included:

- Did you know that you have a _____% chance of losing your life if you're in a gang?
- Did you know gang members are after your family?
- Do you know how many members are killed during initiation?
- What are the requirements for initiation (e.g., kill somebody, beat somebody up, robbery, thefts, extortion)?
- Can you be killed for wearing the wrong color or being in the wrong area?

OUTCOMES

The final layout of the graphic novel will be completed by an illustrator, as yet to be identified. Illustrators are often found via word of mouth or through a local art school. Compensation for an illustrator depends upon whether there is available funding (e.g., grant money), or as an internship for college credit. One other alternative is to offer royalties on the graphic novel if the intention is to publish it and make it available for sale. It usually takes several months for an illustrator to bring the characters to life, with the final formatting and printing left to a publisher. Overall, if the goal is to publish the work, the entire process can take one to two years.

In the meantime, the students were always enthusiastic about the project. As one student summed it up: "This is really cool shit." The teachers at the DJJ school were encouraging and spoke often of the value of the project. They reported that the students looked forward to participating, which was reflected in the words of one student, who said: "Don't take away my privileges to work with the . . . ladies, 'cause I want to work on it." The teachers also reported that students in other classes asked if they could participate.

The overall process was well received by students, teachers, and researchers. There was, however, a difficult situation that arose during the process. One of the students' fathers was killed in jail, and there was speculation that it was a result of gang violence. Our original plan was to meet with the students over a period of about six weeks, but because of the tragic disruption, we were only able to meet with them for four weeks. Despite the time constraints and the sensitivity of the issue, the timing may have been good for the young men to reflect and process the event together and in positive ways. This may explain, at least in part, the ability of the students to develop the story and reach consensus so quickly.

PROCESS SUMMARY

The process described above is summarized in table 4.2. It provides a checklist for steps to take in creating a graphic novel as presented in this chapter, as well as the author's previous experience in creating other graphic novels (Albright & Gavigan, 2014).

The first step is to decide on the style/appearance of the graphic novel. For example, what style do the creators want to use (e.g., superheroes, manga, sports)? The second step could be interchangeable with the first, where the topic or issue is decided. Some topics may lend themselves better to certain styles; for example, the graphic novel about gangs utilized a real-world-type scenario, set in a big city where gangs have an actual presence.

Once the topic and style are determined, the next step is to decide on the story's basic premise. This can be a simple outline of the story, with the creation of the basic characters, location, and time. The next step is to expand the story line and include substantial detail about the story (e.g., how many main characters, basic relationships). Building the characters is the next step. What do they look like? What kind of car do they drive?

Table 4.2. Steps in the process of creating a graphic novel.

	Steps in the Process
1.	Decide on the style/appearance
2.	Decide on the curriculum topic/social issue
3.	Determine story's basic premise
4.	Expand the story line
5.	Develop the characters and dialogue
6.	Block the scenes/determine number of panels and pages
7.	Create illustrations that align with the plot, setting, characters
8.	Provide opportunities for ongoing revisions throughout the process

What kind of family are they from? Brothers? Sisters? What did/do their parents do for a living? This is then followed by the kind of things they say to each other; what dialogue is exchanged between characters.

The next step is to block the scenes, often referred to as storyboarding. This is where the story, characters, and dialogue are brought together in a single panel or over multiple panels. Typically, there are four panels on each page. Through the storyboarding process, it is then possible to determine the total number of panels needed to convey the story, and how many pages there will be in total. The illustrator then brings the characters to life by drawing and coloring the panels, either by hand or using digital technologies, or both. Finally, make sure to review drafts along the way with the creators and other important stakeholders before going to final production.

CONCLUSION

The students who participated in this project worked together to develop an informative and factually accurate resource to help other young adults make informed decisions regarding gangs. They worked well together, despite their differences, which appeared to include different gang memberships, and they were able to arrive at consensus on the story. Based on comments made by both students and teachers, the students were engaged in the process of developing a graphic novel. It gave them an opportunity to share their "expertise" in this area and share stories; while doing so, they were able to make morally sound group judgments and guide each other through difficult decisions, or decisions that might have been more questionable. They appeared pleased with the process and enjoyed participating. It seemed apparent that the school and the students would be interested in making this type of project a permanent part of the curriculum.

APPENDIX A: CHARACTERS IN THE STORY

- Backboy Duke (goes by "Duke")—Spook's best friend—"Back tha Green"—originally from Charleston
- Little Nate—security guard at the jail—brings in contraband—he says, "Stay out of trouble—I ain't gonna keep doing this"—originally from Brooklyn (he won a small lottery and got out of the hood and relocated to Atlanta)
- Pedro—African American/Hispanic—neighborhood cop who arrests Spook and Loco
- Quay—good at stealing from people's houses—originally from West Palm Beach, Florida—teaches Spook and Loco how to steal
- Dre—older guy in the gang
- Julio—dark kind of guy—drug supplier
- Gent—killer—he's already in jail, but that's where Spook will meet him
- Detective Michael Johnson (kind of like Denzel Washington)—another officer—detective who investigates the killings

- Confidential informant (CI)—Kayla Owens—she buys drugs from Julio and tells Officer Pedro
- LB—drug kingpin—lives in Colombia
- Julio (also called J-Lo)—works for LD
- B-Low—another security guard who brings in contraband to the jail—he's a trafficker for LD and sells drugs for LB in prison
- Kev—sells drugs
- J-Bird—crackhead
- C-Loc—LB's right-hand man
- KP—Julio's supplier
- KK—female crackhead
- Jay-Bird—motivator for Spook and Loco—meets them when they get out of jail—he's a lieutenant colonel in the army, an older white male who works in the medical field as a registered nurse

APPENDIX B: LIST OF BLOCKED SCENES

1. Scene: Move to Atlanta with cousin Loco's family
2. Scene: Loco and Spook at school (Spook's new look)
3. Scene: Simone Cortez and Spook meet at school at first football game of the season at the concession stand
4. Scene: Quay, who gets with Spook and Loco to sell drugs; show the three of them talking about dealing drugs (make Spook look uncertain) in a neighborhood
5. Scene: Kayla (CI) snitches on Spook and Loco to Officer Louie
6. Scene: Spook and Loco having conversation with school resource officer (SRO) D. Jenkins
7. Scene: Spook and Loco having conversation with Ashley Jones, guidance counselor
8. Scene: Show relationship between Duke and Quay
9. Scene: Spook and Loco get busted by Officer Louie (dirty cop) at Waffle Spot (a known hangout for the NAPA Boys)
10. Scene: Spook and Loco sentenced to DJJ for two years
11. Scene: Quay kills Officer Louie
12. Scene: Detective Michael Johnson investigates Officer Pedro's death
13. Scene: Simone visits Spook
14. Scene: Loco's family visits Spook and Loco at DJJ
15. Scene: Back to school and at the football game (championship jamboree)—gangs meet (dialogue) and agree to riot at the Waffle Spot parking lot
16. Scene: At the riot—Loco gets shot in the neck in the parking lot, not in a drive-by—physical fighting and handguns
17. Scene: Simone gets shot in the leg (cars are Yukons and Tahoes with rims on; older cars three to four years old)
18. Scene: Hospital
19. Scene: Everybody waiting to hear about Loco
20. Scene: Simone gets bandaged in the ER
21. Scene: Doctor gives the news about Loco
22. Scene: Mr. Jenkins (SRO) and Ashley Jones talking to Loco and Spook in the hospital room
23. Scene: Detective Michael Johnson talking to Spook and Loco in the hospital room about options to go straight
24. Scene: Future, ten years—Loco with Gang Busters; Spook and Simone and baby Gent

REFERENCES

Albright, K. S., & Gavigan, K. (Eds.). (2014). *AIDS in the end zone*. Columbia: University of South Carolina Press.

Axelrod, T. (2015, March 26). Gang violence is on the rise, even as overall violence declines. *U.S. News & World Report*. Retrieved from http://www.usnews.com/news/articles/2015/03/06/gang-violence-is-on-the-rise-even-as-overall-violence-declines.

Botzakis, S. (2009). Graphic novels in education: Cartoons, comprehension, and content knowledge. In D. A. Wooten & B. E. Cullinan (Eds.), *Children's literature in the reading program: An invitation to read* (pp. 15–23). Newark, DE: International Reading Association.

Carter, J. B. (2007). *Building literacy connections with graphic novels: Page by page, panel by panel*. Urbana, IL: National Council of Teachers of English.

CorrectionsOne. (2014). *15 prison tattoos and their meanings*. Retrieved from http://www.correctionsone.com/corrections/articles/7527475-15-prison-tattoos-and-their-meanings.

Federal Bureau of Investigation (FBI). (n.d.). *Gangs*. Retrieved from https://www.fbi.gov/about-us/investigate/vc_majorthefts/gangs.

Gavigan, K. (2012). Sequentially smart: Using graphic novels across the K–12 curriculum. *Teacher Librarian, 39*(5), 20–25.

Monnin, K. (2008). *Perceptions of new literacies with the graphic novel "Bone"* (unpublished doctoral dissertation). Kent, OH: Kent State University.

National Crime Prevention Council. (2016). *Gangs and your child*. Retrieved from http://www.ncpc.org/topics/by-audience/parents/gangs-and-your-child.

National Gang Center. (2012). *National youth gang survey analysis*. Retrieved from http://www.nationalgangcenter.gov/Survey-Analysis.

National Gang Intelligence Center. (2011). *2011 national gang threat assessment: Emerging trends*. Retrieved from https://www.fbi.gov/stats-services/publications/2011-national-gang-threat-assessment/2011-national-gang-threat-assessment-emerging-trends.

Short, J. C., Randolph-Seng, B., & McKenny, A. F. (2013). Graphic presentation: An empirical examination of the graphic novel approach to communicate business concepts. *Business Communication Quarterly, 76*(3), 273–303.

Weissert, W. (2005, August 15). *Family members try to identify bodies of 31 killed in Guatemala prison riots*. Retrieved from http://www.newspapers.com/newspage/115944429/.

Part II

Encouraging Readers

Chapter Five

Call-and-Responsive Reading

Street Literature as Agency for Incarcerated Readers

Vanessa Irvin

"I actually found that education was more democratic in prison. I met people whom I wouldn't have expected to read a lot who did—everybody read. The weird thing is that I read a lot before I got locked up—Chinua Achebe, James Baldwin, anything I could get my hands on. But it was always in my room, or by myself on the train. In prison, nobody would ever question why you were reading" (Betts as cited in Blake, 2010).

INTRODUCTION: LENSES FOR LITERACY

When we think about what makes a literate person in American society, we often refer to the ability to read and write in order to effectively manage lives. The traditional expressions of literacy are needed so that we can read text in order to navigate our movement in public spaces, purchase necessities, and pay bills. I call this ability to read, write, and calculate text and digits "life skills literacy."

However, research shows there is more to literacy than being able to navigate life skills. Literacy is also defined as skills we use to make sense of or to process life events (Heath, 1983) or ways in which we use text to augment and heighten meaning in daily experiences (Street, 1984). Culture and language both play significant roles in the expression of literacy because we express both in various ways depending on regionality and heritage. For example, consider the Philadelphia colloquial term "jawn," which is a placeholder word for any person, place, or thing. This definition is superficial at best because in order to understand the meaning and use of the word "jawn," you would need to understand the Philadelphia regionality, culture, language, and heritage from which "jawn" comes (Nosowitz, 2016). In this vein, literacy is a way of knowing, a way of signifying identity and experience. Literacy is an epistemology. With this understanding, we can begin to think about the ways in which our daily experiences are artifacts that inform our literacy of life. I call this ability to synthesize lived experience "intrinsic literacy."

As readers of our own lived experience, how we intrinsically respond to the environment informs our reading choices in literature, such that reading of our worlds becomes a catalyst for creating and documenting our own narratives. A response to reading informs a response to lived experience and creates a worldview that can be supportive in attaining a deeper understanding of ourselves and our place in the world. This cyclical nature of literary reader response is an important nexus for cognitive and emotional growth, as well as for creating literacy practices that continue to evolve as we mature. This chapter discusses ways in which incarcerated readers' "reading" of personal experience serves as a responsive entry point into reading literature that reflects, clarifies, and renovates their worldview.

THE LITERACY OF LIVING "THE HARD KNOCK LIFE"

Living in low-income city neighborhoods (i.e., the ghetto or the hood) in America is akin to living a "hard knock life" as expressed by Jay-Z's remake of the song "It's a Hard Knock Life" from the Broadway musical *Annie* (Carter, 1998). Indeed, the subtitle to Jay-Z's song is "Ghetto Anthem," which connotes that the struggle and harshness of ghetto life is experienced by its residents. The hard knock life is an identifying aspect of the agency of people who come from the hood. What are the practices of literacy in the hood? What is the literacy of living "the hard knock life?"

Poverty, and the loss of societal access it creates, manifests struggle and harshness from living in a low-income city neighborhood. This hardened reality necessitates literacy practices that involve more than the traditional reading and writing of text. Oftentimes, the daily ways of navigating the streets has more to do with a heightened sense of seeing and responding to nuances in conversation, glances, body language, artwork, architecture, clothing, and even the weather. All these factors can play a deciding role on where you go and whom you interact with at your destination. For example, a dilapidated building may be very useful for some segments of the community; graffiti may be a source of important communication and setting of boundaries. The inner city is a contained environment where localized identifiers determine access and norms that can be the antithesis of the values and norms of mainstream society. In some inner-city settings, localized aesthetics override mainstream societal values and norms as articulated in 24/7 media via television, cinema, music, fashion, and the Internet.

Mainstream society lauds "book smart" citizens. Being "book smart" connotes that if you do Americanism "right," you'll go to school, graduate from college, get a high-paying job, and subscribe to a debt-ridden life in the form of student loans, mortgages, car payments, and taxes. With such responsibilities, you are deemed a productive citizen, seemingly free of harassment from law enforcement, the criminal justice system, and the federal government. On the other hand, if your economic status is such that you do not have access to earning education that makes you "book smart," your literacy practices will be a different set of skills.

Being "street smart" connotes that you are doing Americanism under the radar (so to speak). You'll perhaps graduate from high school and attend some college, but you may not be able to graduate due to financial constraints. You might seek a job in your locale, but infrastructural racism might invariably play a role in how long it takes you to get a job, what position you'll be hired for, what salary you will be paid, and once you have a job how long it will take you to be able to afford to rent or buy a home, and in what neighborhood you can rent or buy. It is fair and necessary to understand that everyone, including low-income citizens, wants to be able to live comfortably, enjoy their families, and take joy in life. "Street smart" low-income citizens use their street literacy practices to strive to achieve and sustain the same "American dream" that mainstream citizens strive to achieve and sustain.

Typically, and all too often, a series of colliding choices and events can lead low-income citizens who are "working the streets" (i.e., employed by the underground economy of selling wares on the streets, out of one's home or car) into opposition with American law enforcement. For example, in her book *The New Jim Crow*, Michelle Alexander (2012) provides an important exploration of American society as a class- and race-based economic system that systematically disenfranchises low-income people of color (pointedly, African American males), which forces citizens to participate in what Venkatesh (2006) names as "the underground economy." The underground economy can be best described as a tax-free exchange system where products are sold on the street at discount prices in the hood. Thus, you can shop for everything from toiletries to holiday gifts to pharmaceuticals. Indeed, it was within the underground economy that street literature, or street lit, arose.

Invariably, merchants are arrested for participating in the entrepreneurial trade of illegal pharmaceuticals and become incarcerated citizens of the U.S. criminal justice system and the prison industrial complex (Alexander, 2012). Oftentimes, low-income young adult citizens participating in the drug trade for survival purposes go from the contained "ethnoracial" environment of the hood to another contained environment, that is, prison (Graaff, 2015). The knowledge that prisoners from inner-city environments possess can be considered a kind of indigenous knowledge where African American and Latino men and women possess a "multidimensional body of understandings that have . . . been viewed by Euroculture as inferior and primitive" (Kincheloe & Steinberg,

2008, p. 136). Indeed, the literacy practices of the urban poor are unique, specific, and particular to a collective and communal lifestyle beyond the boundaries of mainstream social expectations and norms.

Additionally, inner-city citizens are not a monolithic group of hustlers, gangbangers, and prostitutes. Even if they were, we have to remember that hustlers, gangbangers, and prostitutes are complex, multifaceted human beings just like everyone else. Most pointedly, living a low-income urban lifestyle oftentimes amplifies gifts and talents that people are born with because people will utilize their own resources to fill the void of not having things that money can buy. The resourcefulness of a poverty lifestyle conveys literacy practices that employ complex approaches to navigating the social fabric of inner-city living. It's important for us to remember and understand that low-income and homeless people are also writers, artists, musicians, dancers, financiers, and whatever other God-given gifts, talents, and interests they inherently possess, regardless of any other agency due to financial dire straits. Regardless of income, citizens are always employing their ways of knowing in their daily lives. These identity constructs are fully expressed in character development throughout street fiction.

While pounding the pavement requires focusing on a set of social practices that enables citizens to successfully navigate the streets, the regimented confinement of prison life requires another set of practices particular to that setting. Whereas sociocultural forms of reading and writing may have been a focus for navigating life skills in the hood, within the confined walls of prisons, where daily life is regimented according to penal expectations of the criminal justice system, traditional forms of reading and writing may come into fuller play in prisoners' daily living and survival practices (Graaff, 2015; Sweeney, 2010). Also, as a form of psychological survival, reading, writing, and the fine arts become a reflective space in which self-rehabilitation, in resistance to the dehumanizing nature of prison life, emerges.

FROM THE STREETS TO PRISON: READER RESPONSE TO STREET LITERATURE

During the late 1990s, a popular wave of fiction was being published and distributed on the streets of Harlem, Philadelphia, Baltimore, Chicago, and Atlanta, to name a few. These books were novels about daily life in the hood. Considered a renaissance of the pulp fiction novel movement during the blaxploitation film era of the early to mid-1970s, works such as *The Coldest Winter Ever* (Souljah, 1996), *Flyy Girl* (Tyree, 1996), and *True to the Game* (Woods, 1999) were reminiscent of the works of 1970s pulp fiction authors Donald Goines and Iceberg Slim. These hip-hop-era novels were raw, gritty stories about love, life, crime, and coming-of-age in the hood. Written with engaging, relatable characters, plots, language, and prose, with settings in recognizable, live streets, these books lit a fire for youth and adult inner-city readers and inspired a new reading generation of people who had never read before (Morris, Agosto, Hughes-Hassell, & Cottman, 2006).

Quickly, more authors came to the forefront, writing and publishing this new genre called urban fiction or street lit. Teen readers were visiting public libraries and borrowing the books, and then passing them among one another, so that multiple people read the same book within one circulation cycle (Morris et al., 2006). Sweeney (2010) reports that incarcerated women were doing the same kind of communal reading-borrowing-sharing cycle with the limited street lit books that they could check out from the prison library. Also during this time, incarcerated citizens began writing their stories from inside prison walls and having them published by fellow authors living out in society. One relationship that is well known for this collaboration is Teri Woods and Kwame Teague. Woods was author and publisher of Teri Woods Publishing, and she sponsored publication of quick-rising author and prisoner Kwame Teague's very popular (now classic) Dutch series (Brown, 2011; Irvin Morris, 2012). Quite a few popular street lit authors who became mainstream sensations wrote from their prison cells and experienced literary success upon release (e.g., Vicki Stringer, Wahida Clark, Shannon Holmes, Relentless Aaron, and J. M. Benjamin, to name a few).

Graaff (2015) identifies the connection between the streets and prison as a kind of "symbiosis." In her book *Street Literature: Black Popular Fiction in the Era of U.S. Mass Incarceration*, Graaff discusses the production of street literature on the streets and the production of street literature in prisons as "narrative locations" where "streets and prisons are interconnected on a social, structural, and cultural level in characters' everyday experiences and practices" (p. 133). Graaff contends that there is an interweaving between literary spaces in street lit novels (i.e., identifying real-life locations and events within a fictionalized story) and narrative spaces of street lit authors' and readers' lived lives on the streets and in prison life.

Indeed, within literary theory, the street lit novel can be situated as a naturalistic novel where experience trumps imagination with observation and analysis as data for creating narrative or fictionalized drama (Zola, 1967). Henry James reminds us of the following:

> The power to guess the unseen from the seen, to trace the implication of things, to judge the whole piece by the pattern, the condition of feeling life in general so completely that you are well on your way to knowing any particular corner of it—this cluster of gifts may almost be said to constitute experience, and they occur in country and in town, and in the most differing stages of education. If experience consists of impressions, it may be said that impressions *are* experience, just as . . . they are the very air we breathe. (1967, p. 396)

The synergy between the lived experiences of street lit authors and readers on the streets and in prison is an ongoing documentation of living and reflecting on that lifestyle across staged platforms. The street is a stage and the prison is a stage, where performance to navigate experience can often be a conscription based on structural confinements that exist in both places. For the street, law enforcement confines behavior and experience based on "ethnoracial" hegemonic social structure of a mainstream Eurocentric American society (Graaff, 2015). Prison experience is a confinement based on a punitive system of pseudorehabilitation that is based on the same hegemonic racial structure that dehumanizes the dignity of incarcerated citizens (Sweeney, 2010).

With these dynamics in mind, an incarcerated citizen reading a street lit novel is reminded of what life was like on the outside (the streets), although it may be similar to the confines of what life is like on the inside (prison). This infusion of fiction with reality is what Michelle Citron (1999) calls a "necessary fiction," where experience serves as an opportunity to reevaluate "prevailing norms from their functional contexts," as reading response theorist Wolfgang Iser (1978, p. 74) says. Iser calls the kind of cyclical call-and-reading-response that occurs with incarcerated street lit readers a "literary recodification of social and historical norms" (p. 74) such that readers see/read what they normally cannot see during the distractedness of daily living. Meaning comes from the reader's reconciliation of the text with his or her own lived experiences. This reading response becomes "transformed memory" (p. 111).

We cannot expect people to erase their experiences or to negate their experiences as if they never occurred at all, or that whatever acts or experiences that happened are to be forgotten. Indigenous knowledge is the intrinsic epistemology of lived experience within history, context, and culture. As such, such knowledge becomes a literacy practice, an everyday act of living that is based on what is iteratively seen, felt, experienced, and known. Street literature in its twenty-first-century iteration is a strong documentation of orality, activity, belief, and historical manifestation of some cultural expressivities that cannot be denied or swept under the rug of academic or cultural embarrassment. It is what it is. Street literature, its authors and readers, on the streets and in prisons is not the only representation of African American or Latino American culture. However, it is an aspect of our culture that needs to be unpacked and understood.

In this vein, librarians have been working to respect urban fiction that is read and requested by library users throughout the United States. The Street Literature Book Award Medal (SLBAM) was instituted in 2009 to document what library *readers* are enjoying about street literature. Who are the readers reading? What are readers deeming as so-called quality literature? Believe it or not, what readers in the world want to read and choose to read is often not too far left of what authors are writing and having published. Within contemporary street literature, it has been my observation that as the authors have matured in their narratives so have the readers matured in their reading interests and tastes. Indeed, with social media as an immediate medium in which authors and readers can readily interact and give one another feedback, in today's times, the genre is being cowritten by readers and authors in very nuanced ways that have made the genre a constant conversation between the real and the fictive. The SLBAM awards are a conduit through which readers inform authors of their preferences, and librarians mediate that conversation with fieldwork to report circulation data and readers' responses to authors and book titles. Librarians and other educators can use the SLBAM awards (located at www.streetliterature.com) as a resource to share vetted authors and titles for the street literature genre.

CONCLUSION: RESPECTING THE READING LIVES OF INCARCERATED READERS

This chapter has attempted to explain the agency of incarcerated readers reading street literature. Even though literacy practices of inner-city citizens are typically nontraditional (as in not necessarily a voracious reading population among people active in the underground and illegal economy), we must respectfully acknowledge the innovative and courageous ways in which incarcerated readers and writers avidly embrace traditional literacy practices as part of navigating the challenges of prison life. The ways that prisoners have written and read back to their own experiences, via the writing and reading of street literature as a reflection of their lived experiences, speaks to a resiliency in creative expression. Even while there is reportage of a lack of resources in prisons due to security policies and regulations, and recognizing the limitations of reading materials and reading culture in prison libraries, it is vital that we have a solid understanding of the importance of incarcerated readers being able to read and write what they want to read and write, when and however they can. To support reading practices of incarcerated citizens, book titles vetted via the SLBAM awards can be a means through which materials can be added to prison library collections.

Just as social practices on the streets become an indigenous literacy that makes a person a reader of experience, therefore "street smart," literary practices in prison can gravitate a person's interest to become a reader of literature, therefore "book smart." It is no surprise that incarcerated readers and writers come out of prison back into society as successful entrepreneurs and authors with mainstream publishers. As earlier discussed, some of the most popular and well-regarded street literature authors today began their careers while in prison, chronicling their memories and recording comrades' lifestyles as narratives of action, adventure, romance, fantasy, and redemption.

In the realm of education, literacy has to take a broad definition to include the impacts of living life, and not just the impacts of rote reading, writing, and arithmetic as part of the concept, framework, and idea for "literacy" and the "practices" such ways of knowing bring. Particularly in this twenty-first century of social media and the additional literary practices that occur online, experience is now privileging imagination in very concrete ways. Thus, we must give credit and credence to incarcerated readers because their reading habits are informing their lives in edifying and empowering ways, at a time in history where naturalistic fiction is creating an entire literary corpus that is culturally and socially generated and historically based. We cannot censor anyone's collective readings and writings of life. To do so would be to negate the very gifts and talents that manifest themselves in all of us, always.

Yet, incarcerated youths may not have access to social media or other means of contemporary digital reading platforms (e.g., e-books); or if they do, they may be heavily filtered, creating barriers to open access to information and leisure reading options. With these limitations in mind, one strategy that can be employed to enhance reading interests is to utilize professional tools such as the aforementioned SLBAM booklists, located on the streetliterature.com website. The SLBAM awards are conferred yearly, giving recognition to the most-read urban literature titles by library patrons across the United States. A committee of librarians ethnographically collect data on the reading interests and trends of their library patrons who request and read street lit. Conferred since 1999, the SLBAM award lists are valuable resources for locating relatable fiction and nonfiction titles that reflect urban city living in contemporary times.

Another useful tool for locating meaningful texts for incarcerated youth and adults is Library Services for Youth in Custody (LSYC). LSYC is an organization that advocates for meaningful and accessible library materials for incarcerated and at-risk youth (see http://www.youthlibraries.org). The LSYC sponsors the In the Margins booklist, which is annually announced, based on a librarian committee that selects fiction, nonfiction, and a top ten list of titles. The In the Margins lists are available on LSYC's website, youthlibraries.org. In addition to the In the Margins booklists, the LSYC offers booklists for graphic novels, poetry, and many other topics and genres. Utilizing titles offered via SLBAM and In the Margins, teachers and librarians working with incarcerated youth can pique their readers' interest in text of various formats. Regardless of setting, readers can become communal and collaborative about their reading preferences and habits, often talking with like-minded readers, sharing reading responses and strategies (Irvin Morris, 2012; Sweeney, 2010). The SLBAM and LSYC resources can be vital conduits for creating interactive reading and writing groups using street/urban literature as a tool for calling readers to respond to relatable stories that heighten and enhance their literacy practices.

For such initiatives to be truly impactful and sustainable, it is imperative for educators to take an earnest interest in reading the books that their students choose to read. It behooves social workers, counselors, librarians, and teachers working with at-risk youth to read what their teens read, and also to read stories that reflect their students' lived lives. When service providers read stories that convey a better understanding of their students' or clients' experiences, their responses to their youths' needs can become more culturally competent, and in turn, youths respond to reading in ways that can make them lifelong readers, writers, and learners.

I close with the request that we reperceive incarcerated readers as whole human beings with gifts, talents, interests, beliefs, and habits that are valuable and need space and place to root and grow. Reading inspires the work of that inner rootedness and growth. Writing records memory of experience, be it joyful or traumatic. Everyone has the right to read and write their own lives into memory and history. Educators everywhere must be relentless to support the natural endeavors of incarcerated readers as literate citizens. In practical terms, practitioners who ensure open and equal access to urban/street literature of various topics, categories, and formats provide an invaluable information service and advocacy for street literature as a valid approach to signifying agency and identity for incarcerated readers.

REFERENCES

Alexander, M. (2012). *The new Jim Crow: Mass incarceration in the age of colorblindness*. New York, NY: New Press.

Blake, M. (2010, November 30). The exchange: R. Dwayne Betts on prison, poetry, and justice. *New Yorker*. Retrieved from http://www.newyorker.com/books/page-turner/the-exchange-r-dwayne-betts-on-prison-poetry-and-justice

Brown, E. (Ed.). (2011, July 30). 8 urban fiction authors who overcame prison and forged lucrative careers. *Atlanta Post*. Retrieved from http://atlantapost.com/2011/07/30/8-urban-fiction-authors-who-overcame-prison-and-forged-lucrative-careers/8/

Carter, S. (Jay-Z). (1998). *Vol. 2, Hard knock life*. New York, NY: Roc-A-Fella Records.

Citron, M. (1999). *Home movies and other necessary fictions* (*Visible evidence*, Vol. 4). Minneapolis: University of Minnesota Press.

Graaff, K. (2015). *Street literature: Black popular fiction in the era of U.S. mass incarceration* (American Studies Monograph Series, 263). Heidelberg, Germany: Universitätsverlag Winter.

Heath, S. B. (1983). *Ways with words: Language, life and work in communities and classrooms*. Cambridge, UK: Cambridge University Press.

Irvin Morris, V. (2012). *The readers' advisory guide to street literature*. Chicago, IL: ALA Editions.

Iser, W. (1978). *The act of reading: A theory of aesthetic response*. Baltimore, MD: John Hopkins University Press.

James, H. (1967). On writing from experience. In P. Stevick (Ed.), *The theory of the novel* (p. 396). New York, NY: Free Press.

Kincheloe, J. L., & Steinberg, S. R. (2008). Indigenous knowledges in education: Complexities, dangers, and profound benefits. In N. K. Denzin, Y. S. Lincoln, & L. T. Smith (Eds.), *Handbook of critical and indigenous methodologies* (pp. 135–156). Thousand Oaks, CA: Sage.

Morris, V. J., Agosto, D. P., Hughes-Hassell, S., & Cottman, D. T. (2006). Street lit: Flying off teen fiction bookshelves in Philadelphia public libraries. *Journal of Young Adult Library Service, 5*(1), 16–23.

Nosowitz, D. (2016, March 24). The enduring mystery of "jawn," Philadelphia's all-purpose noun according to experts, it's unlike any word, in any language. *The Atlas Obscura*. Retrieved from http://www.atlasobscura.com/articles/the-enduring-mystery-of-jawn-philadelphias-allpurpose-noun

Souljah, S. (1996). *The coldest winter ever: A novel*. New York: NY: Simon & Schuster.

Street, B. V. (1984). *Literacy in theory and practice* (Cambridge Studies in Oral and Literate Culture). Cambridge, UK: Cambridge University Press.

Sweeney, M. (2010). *Reading is my window: Books and the art of reading in women's prisons*. Chapel Hill: University of North Carolina Press.

Tyree, O. (1996). *Flyy girl: An urban classic novel*. New York, NY: Simon & Schuster.

Venkatesh, S. (2006). *Off the books: The underground economy of the urban poor*. Cambridge, MA: Harvard University Press.

Woods, T. (1999). *True to the game: A Teri Woods fable*. Havertown, PA: Meow Meow.

Zola, E. (1967). Experience and the naturalistic novel. In P. Stevick (Ed.), *The theory of the novel* (pp. 394–395). New York, NY: Free Press.

Chapter Six

Books behind the Fence

Susan McNair

"Reading gives us somewhere to go when we have to stay where we are" (Cooley as cited in Angelo, 2014).

Bob looked astonished after I told him we had the complete House of Night (Cast & Cast, 2007–2014) series. Fairly new to our school, I had only seen this slight young man a few times, but he was visibly excited about the new series' editions on display with the other new books. The rest of the forty-five-minute period went well as students checked out books and read magazines.

As I tidied the library in preparation for my next class, I discovered six empty magazine covers on the back table and only four magazines. I immediately knew the missing magazines were *People* (very popular for the often scantily clad beautiful women), but I counted the magazines to be certain. I went to the classroom to confront the students; while no one admitted taking the magazines, Bob did offer to come back to the library to help me look. I said that would work only if "you know exactly where the magazines are." From previous experience, I felt sure he had the magazines. If he went back with me to search, he would be able to hide and then find the magazines he had stolen. Security searched the students, and Bob did have the two magazines. Days "behind the fence" are often a roller coaster of such highs and lows.

This chapter will explore how I changed the function of the library, from being used for study hall and receiving very few student visits, to a friendly, literary, and literacy-rich hub. I will discuss how a school library "behind the fence" is both similar and dissimilar to a traditional school library. Topics explored will include collection development and arrangement, schedules, information access, and material control.

DIFFERENCE BETWEEN SCHOOL AND DETENTION LIBRARIES

While education is the top priority in schools, this is not the case in juvenile institutions, where safety must be the number one concern. Safety is a multifaceted issue: the youth have been incarcerated for the safety of the general public, and everyone located "behind the fence," including the incarcerated youth, must be kept safe. Safety issues impact education in a variety of ways; for example, Internet access is tightly controlled. In addition to ensuring that students do not visit inappropriate sites, we must be certain they never contact a victim or post any information on social media. Also, it is imperative that some students not be in close proximity to other students, making scheduling classes more complex.

Listed below are a few of the safety concerns in a juvenile facility:

1. No matter how engaging the student, always remember he or she was incarcerated for a reason.
2. Be alert, and remember where you are at all times.
3. If something or someone makes you feel uncomfortable, respect that feeling.
4. Never leave anything that could be a weapon where students can access it.
5. Put away pens and markers. Students use them to tag buildings and themselves with gang graffiti.

6. Do not share personal information or pictures with the students.

CREATING A STUDENT-CENTERED LIBRARY

I believe the single most important component of a successful library program is the librarian. You can have a beautiful building and an outstanding, extensive collection, but if no one is there to provide friendly and knowledgeable service to patrons, the library will never be fully utilized. Juvenile detention facilities are not naturally happy places, so I always strive to be upbeat and smiling when I greet my students. They know I enjoy talking with them about books and helping them find information or something special to read.

Respect is crucial in any relationship, and especially so "behind the fence." These students are very conscious of any slight, or of being treated with disrespect by another person. I treat each of them with the same attitude of respect that I expect from them in return, and I do not allow them to disrespect each other while in the library. I always listen to whatever they want to share, but I never pry into their personal lives, backgrounds, or charges. Previously, I worked in a large public high school for thirteen years, and other than the need for closer observation, I treat these students as I treated my former students. Within the school, I believe it is crucial that the youth are always seen as students first and incarcerated juveniles second. When I discuss our book collection with students wanting more adult-themed books, I always remind them they are in a school library. They tend to forget this and identify our space as a prison library where they believe adult materials would be available, and I want them to see the library as an educational facility with appropriate materials for secondary school students.

On one of my first days, I was surprised to hear students call each other juveniles, a derogatory reference to their status as incarcerated youth. In fact, a student recently thanked me for calling them students. During one class, several students created a disturbance in the library and had to be removed by officers. Once all the commotion was over, I complimented the remaining students on their positive behavior by saying, "Students, I want to thank you for your excellent behavior during this disturbance. It is always nice to have students who know how to conduct themselves properly." One replied, "Thank you for not calling us juveniles." I replied, "You are my students." A little respect goes a long way toward building positive relationships with these marginalized young adults.

ARRANGING THE PHYSICAL SPACE

Before my arrival, the school had been without a certified librarian for several years. The library was used as a study hall to hold classes when a teacher was absent, and an associate teacher sometimes checked out books. New books had been ordered by the principal and received, but no one knew how to catalog and process them. There were no magazine subscriptions, and the library was crowded with tables and chairs to accommodate multiple classes.

My first goal was to create a student-centered library. To be more accessible to students and to provide better supervision, I moved the circulation desk from the library office into the main library. I loaned tables and chairs to other rooms in the school to create a more spacious and open appearance. I added plants and moved the upholstered chairs from the office I hardly ever use to the main part of the library to form a comfortable student reading area. I took down the old, tired decorations and created tree and leaf decorations for the theme "Branching Out at Your Library." Students mainly requested urban fiction, and I wanted to introduce them to multiple genres and authors. I made limbs from brown bulletin board paper for each of the different genres and created colorful leaves with names of the authors who wrote in that genre and hung these above the fiction shelves.

During this redecorating process, the library was open for student use. Student comments were positive about the changes I was making. One remarked, "I used to hate to come to the library, but now I like it." Music to my ears! Once I fashioned a more comfortable, relaxed atmosphere, I began processing the new books stored in the library office. Students responded favorably to the revamping of the library, new books, and the presence of full-time professional library services by increasing our library circulations by 250 percent in less than three years.

Students often say, "I brought back your library book." Or, "I left your library book in the dorm." I always respond with, "These are not my books; these are *our* books." My goal is for students to take ownership of the library and materials and see them as belonging to the school and its students, not to me. I think a shared culture of ownership is essential for helping students take pride in their school and to encourage them to care for and return our library books.

STUDENT LIBRARY VISITS

New books had not been added to the library's collection for several years, so word of their availability spread quickly. As students entered, they asked, "Where are the new books?" The library was on a flexible schedule, and a teacher could send three students to the library for twenty minutes. Since classes are scheduled to keep certain students separated, only one teacher could send students at a time. Soon there was not enough time in the day for all the students who wanted to visit the library to have an opportunity to come. Students would see me in the hall and tell me how they wanted to come to the library, but it was always full. A wonderful problem!

While I was seeking a solution for how to ensure all students had the opportunity to come to the library, we made several overall school changes, and the library had to move to a fixed schedule. I had very mixed feelings about this change, but it has proven to be a positive one for students. As with all changes, there were pros and cons. With the flexible schedule, some students used the library as a quiet refuge from constant interaction with other students and adults. However, not all students got to come to the library. Some students did not like to ask teachers for a library pass. As in any school setting, troublesome students often get frequent permission to go to the library. With the fixed schedule, all students are guaranteed a forty-five-minute library visit each week. However, students may not want or need to come to the library at the weekly assigned time. I work with security, teachers, and administrators to ensure voracious readers have the opportunity to exchange books as needed.

During library visits, students have the opportunity to check out books and read current magazines. *People* and *Sports Illustrated* are the library's most popular magazines, and students also enjoy *ESPN*, *Entertainment Weekly*, *Ebony*, *Car and Driver*, *Cycle World*, and *Dirt Bikes*. We subscribe to *Teen Vogue* and *Seventeen* for the girls, but I keep them in my office when the boys' classes visit to ensure they do not tear out pictures of the attractive females. I economize by not subscribing to a daily newspaper since students did not read it. I bring students my Sunday newspapers, and they especially enjoy the sales flyers. I am careful to remove any flyers advertising weapons and the obituaries, as students may learn of the death of a relative or friend before a family member or social worker has broken the news.

Also, I keep a table of books (*Ripley's Believe It or Not*; *Guinness World Records*; art books; and coffee-table-style books on sports, cars, and animals) that cannot be checked out, but students can browse while in the library. Students enjoy sharing the interesting and odd facts from these books. Sometimes the entire group will be drawn into the discussion, and I have the opportunity to provide additional information and resources on a topic of interest. Some of these books are large, and security prefers that large volumes not be sent to the dorms. Keeping these popular and often more expensive books in the library ensures a longer life and greater access for the books. Once a *Ripley's* or *Guinness* book goes to the dorm, I have found it next to impossible to get it returned.

I am not a stickler about a silent library and encourage students to share information. Often the talk is not about library books, but as long as it is not overly loud, profane, or about their offenses, neither teachers nor I restrict it. I use this opportunity to reinforce acceptable decorum standards for when they will be "outside the fence," and we have had many debates about how the First Amendment does not grant carte blanche protection to those uttering profanities.

Students are not allowed unsupervised use of computers, and the library only has one computer—at my desk. I conduct Internet searches with students on topics ranging from requirements for military enlistment to religion to animals to background information on books they are reading, and I use this opportunity to model effective search strategies. Like other libraries, we use the Internet to find and print information on topics that are not covered by our book collection.

FICTION BY GENRE

When I arrived, the library was arranged in the traditional manner according to the Dewey Decimal System. Students would ask me for a mystery book, and I would begin by showing them Caroline Cooney, then Lois Duncan, followed by John Grisham. Before I could get to James Patterson, their eyes had glazed over, and they had lost interest. To increase student buy-in to our library culture, I began talking with them about how they would like the fiction collection to be arranged. Everyone I spoke with wanted the books to be shelved together by genre. I immediately began reorganizing the fiction collection using various colored dots to denote the different genres and creating signage to explain the color-coded system. I had two goals for this project:

1. To make it easier for students to find books they wanted
2. To encourage students to broaden their reading selections

Since most books are not exclusively one genre, assigning a genre to individual books proved to be a challenging task. To satisfy student demand, I needed to have a large urban fiction collection, so I allocated romance and realistic fiction set in an urban environment to the urban fiction collection. As we have a small population of girls, having a limited romance collection is not a problem. The small number of female students gives me time to assist each girl individually and help them find romance books shelved in realistic and urban fiction. I want readers to expand their reading horizons and try different genres, so I created a natural flow of themes in the genre arrangement. For example, I shelved the realistic fiction beside the door in hopes of catching students' attention as they enter, and as a natural lead-in to urban fiction. Given urban fiction's popularity and its tendency to disappear from the shelves, I did not want to shelve it next to the door.

Students quickly learned the new genre system and the color dots of their favorite genres, and I often hear them helping each other to find the section they want. Now when students want to find a mystery, I take them to the mystery section, point out a few of the best titles, and allow them to browse. They enjoy being more independent in making their book selections, and they will often pull up a chair in front of their favorite genre to read multiple book cover blurbs. Loss of the ability to make personal choices is a natural element of incarceration, so the freedom to choose and read what you want is even more important to these youths than to the usual library patron.

As is typical with most incarcerated youth, over two-thirds of our students' reading levels are two or more grade levels behind as measured by our last two administrations of the MAP (Measures of Academic Progress) test. As with all struggling readers, it is essential to provide books with themes relevant to their life experiences. Until I get a feel for an individual student's comfortable reading level, I usually recommend books on varying reading levels and encourage the student to read a little of each book while in the library.

Circulation has continued to climb in the eighteen months since I rearranged the library fiction collection by genre. Our fewer than 125 students have checked out 2,657 books, an average of 148 books per month. As in any library, I have some students who check out a lot of books and other students who never check out anything. Fiction comprises the majority of our checkouts, making up 87 percent. During their library visits, students often read and look at nonfiction books, but they tend to check out fiction books to take back to the dorms. Figure 6.1 compares the number of copies in each genre to the number of student checkouts. The library's fantasy collection was very large when I arrived, and it has the largest discrepancy between number of copies and circulations, although it does have a devoted, albeit small, group of readers. Of course, most of our fantasy collection is contained in series, which necessitates additional copies.

COLLECTION DEVELOPMENT

When I became librarian, the collection was in desperate need of weeding, but I did not want to sort through too much until I knew my students' preferences and my teachers' needs. I weeded nonfiction titles based on book condition and age relevancy and fiction titles based on book condition and age appropriateness. I predominantly weeded books that were too childish for our students, along with older, unappealing copies. I have since weeded a second time based on student usage and to improve the appearance of the collection.

Our school population averages between 100–120 students ages thirteen through nineteen, with 88 percent being male and 79 percent being African American. These students have a wide variety of reading tastes, and student requests comprise the majority of our book orders. I believe student input encourages ownership and is crucial to quality collection development, and I have always solicited recommendations from students as to what books to purchase. Student suggestions are subjected to the same scrutiny as any other book purchase, and students often request books that are either too sexually graphic or too violent for our school library. I make a point of following up with the student who requested the book to explain why I am not ordering that book. Usually, the student disagrees with my assessment, but there are certain books that do not belong in our library. In addition to requests for specific fiction books and authors, books on such diverse topics as fatherhood, meditation, paranormal experiences, the NBA, dirt bikes, African religions, secret societies, and realistic graphic novels were contained in recent orders.

I do not order books as they are requested, but I combine requested books with those I have selected into several large orders a year. The purchasing process of a state agency is cumbersome, and small orders are impractical. Unfortunately, by the time a requested book has been ordered, received, and processed, sometimes the student has transferred to a step-down facility or has been paroled. However, the requested book usually finds an audience with other students.

Just like student recommendations, donations must be subject to the same criteria as purchases. For some inexplicable reason, people seem to think we are so desperate for reading matter that we will accept absolutely any donation of printed materials. An elderly lady called one day and offered me her lifetime collection of *Southern Living* magazine. Just what every teenage boy wants to read! I have also been given boxes of children's books. I do believe read-alouds are a great way to introduce new classroom topics, so I added the relevant texts to our collection.

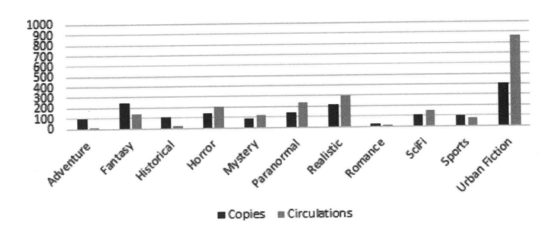

Figure 6.1. Comparison of number of copies to number of circulations. *Susan McNair, chapter author.*

URBAN FICTION

When I was new to the facility, multiple students asked me for books by Zane. They were very surprised when I replied, "We both know that Zane writes urban erotica, and it is not appropriate in a high school library." They argued, "We are in prison." I responded with, "Right now, you are in our school library." I think it is important for students to believe that education is education, no matter the location, and this also allows me to reinforce the concept of a shared school library.

However, a library collection must be well matched to its patrons, and I do order much more edgy and streetwise books than I purchased for my former large, rural high school library. In two and a half years, I have added 270 copies of urban fiction titles to our collection in response to student demand. It is a balancing act to acquire books that do not glorify a gang lifestyle and still appeal to incarcerated youth, many of whom are involved with gangs.

Often, regular review sources do not include urban fiction, and more nontraditional sources need to be consulted. Urban fiction was not a popular genre at my previous school, and I knew I needed to quickly bring myself up to speed. *The Readers' Advisory Guide to Street Literature* by Vanessa Irvin Morris (2012) has been an invaluable guide for learning the characteristics of urban fiction and popular authors and titles. Several online resources I use are included in the recommendations for further reading at the end of this chapter.

POPULAR NONFICTION

Many of our students are artistically gifted and are interested in drawing and music books to help them hone these skills. Books on how to rap, including beats and rhyming dictionaries, are also in high demand. I have been surprised by how popular poetry books are behind the fence, and I am constantly adding new titles to our poetry collection. Books of poetry by youth or adults who are or have been incarcerated are of particular interest.

We are all interested in people whose experiences mirror our own, and my students are no exception. Biographies and memoirs, especially about and by people who have been incarcerated, are frequently requested by our students. With these books, it is important to look at the impact of the person's entire life, not just the crime for which that person was incarcerated. For example, we have two different memoirs by Tookie Williams, the founder of the Crips who was executed for murder. However, he turned his life around while in prison and became an antidrug, antigang advocate who was nominated for the Nobel Peace Prize. While I am sure my students are very interested in the gang-related parts of the memoirs, they are also exposed to the positive aspects of Williams's life and how a prison sentence does not have to define a life. Our school purpose statement is "Individualizing instruction that leads to positive and productive lives." I do this in the library by providing literature that is entertaining for pleasure reading and also by providing materials that encourage students to examine their lives and make more positive decisions. As with all books, it is crucial that the tone be realistic and not didactic.

Given the success of organizing fiction by genre, I am undertaking a similar project in our biography section, which is currently arranged by alphabet. This current arrangement does not meet the needs of students who usually ask questions like, "Where are our books about rap musicians?" We then go through the same scenario as we did with finding mysteries. I am organizing our biographies by categories of the persons' accomplishments in order to expedite students' finding a particular book while also encouraging browsing.

Circulation policies, as listed below, must take into account students being incarcerated in a residential facility:

1. Check with security to determine how many books students can have in their rooms.
2. I do everything I can to facilitate students' exchanging library books. If students forget their book and promise to bring it after lunch or the next day, I hold the new book they selected and take it to one of their classes to exchange books with them.
3. Coordinate with security officers and teachers to allow prolific readers extra opportunities to exchange library books.

4. I am not concerned about overdue books, just getting books returned.
5. Books are sometimes damaged in dorms due to circumstances beyond the borrower's control, so I do not charge students for damaged/lost books
6. Partner with security for assistance with getting books returned from dorms.
7. Partner with the agency office responsible for discharging students when they are transferred or paroled to have library books added to the list of state-owned property to be returned.

ADVOCACY

The library is a singular component of educational services, which is a small part of the much larger correctional facility. It is crucial the library never be lost within the concerns of the larger entities. As in all libraries, it is incumbent on the librarian to advocate for and to promote the library's agenda. I ensure my principal and superintendent know of the library's successes and needs through a monthly report that includes circulation data and major events and projects in the library, along with school-wide tasks I am accomplishing. Schools behind the fence tend to be much smaller than regular schools, meaning there are fewer teachers to serve on committees and complete ancillary tasks. I have always been a team player and volunteer for select committees and jobs that allow me to develop closer relationships with faculty and staff and keep the library program in the forefront of the school. These extra duties are time consuming, but do enhance my, and the library's, value and strengthen the validity of funding requests.

CLOSING

I opened this chapter with a quotation by Mason Cooley: "Reading gives us somewhere to go when we have to stay where we are" (as cited in Angelo, 2014). My students have to "stay where they are" and desperately need "somewhere to go." Helping them find that vital, if temporary, mental escape through books is the most challenging and demanding job of my career, but also the most rewarding.

REFERENCES

Angelo, C. (2014). *28 Quotes to remind you to never stop reading.* Retrieved from http://thoughtcatalog.com/courtney-angelo/2014/08/28-quotes-to-remind-you-to-never-stop-reading/
Cast, P. C., & Cast, K. (2007–2014). House of Night series. New York: St. Martin's Griffin.
Irvin Morris, V. (2012). *The readers' advisory guide to street literature.* Chicago, IL: American Library Association.

RESOURCES FOR FURTHER READING

Genrifying Fiction

Goldblatt, N. (2015). One easy decision: Genre-classified fiction. *Library Media Connection, 5,* 20–22.
Jackman, B. (2014). GenreShelving: Why and how I made the leap. *Library Media Connection, 5,* 22–24.
Mrs. Reader Pants. (n.d.). The Library Genre-fication Project. Retrieved from http://www.readerpants.net/2011/09/genre-fication-project.html

Urban Fiction

Colorado State Library. (n.d.). Library Services for Youth in Custody. Retrieved from http://www.youthlibraries.org
Morris, V. (n.d.). *Street literature . . . bringing you the word on the street & urbanity.* Retrieved from http://www.streetliterature.com
Ribay, R. (2013). What makes a good YA urban fiction novel. *The Horn Book, 6,* 48–54.
Street Fiction: Author interviews, news and reviews of urban books. (n.d.). Retrieved from http://streetfiction.org

Chapter Seven

Creating a Community of Writers Using Graphic Novels

Karen Gavigan

"Writing, I think, is not apart from living. Writing is a kind of double living. The writer experiences everything twice. Once in reality and once in that mirror which waits always before or behind" (Bowen, 1957).

It is estimated that 2.18 million young adults under the age of eighteen are arrested each year in the United States. In addition, nearly 93,000 of these youth are in public and private detention and correctional institutions (Sickmund & Puzzanchera, 2014). The literacy skills of these incarcerated youth have consistently been identified as academically weaker than those of nonincarcerated youth their same age. For example, Brunner (1993) found that 89 percent of students housed in correctional facilities required remediation in reading and writing skills. In terms of written language skills, Foley (2001) determined that young adults who were incarcerated were significantly less competent than their peers who were not. Specifically, Drakeford (2002) found that incarcerated youth performed poorly on standardized writing tests, had more difficulty with writing compositions, and used poor sentence construction in their writing.

Unfortunately, the challenges of teaching writing skills to incarcerated youth are not limited to the academic limitations of this at-risk population. For example, it is difficult to design and implement quality writing programs in correctional facilities, since the average stay for incarcerated youth is between fifteen and thirty-seven days (Snyder & Sickmund, 1999). In addition, given that the time spent with students is often brief, educators may choose to emphasize reading more than writing activities in their instruction. Further, incarcerated students often have low writing efficacy, since they may have experienced lingering academic and behavioral difficulties in former educational settings.

Effective written language instruction that promotes academic achievement is needed to improve the overall literacy skills of incarcerated youth. One way to meet the writing needs of incarcerated youth is to expand the definition of literacy. For example, associations such as the American Association of School Librarians (AASL), the National Council of Teachers of English (NCTE), and the International Reading Association (IRA) have added visual literacy to their standards in an effort to meet the needs of today's twenty-first-century learners. Visual literacy is the ability to recognize and understand ideas illustrated with images or pictures (Cummings, Bardack, & Gonsoulin, 2010).

Graphic novels are increasingly recognized by educators as an engaging visual literacy format that can meet the informational and recreational needs of today's learners. As Weiner (2004) states, graphic novels can serve "as transitions into more print-intensive works, enticing reluctant readers into prose books and, in some cases, offering literary experiences that linger in the mind long after the book is finished" (p. 115). Given their popularity and wide range of genres, graphic novels can motivate at-risk students to write in new and creative ways. They are powerful literacy tools that can be used to engage incarcerated youth in a variety of writing experiences. This chapter will introduce best practices for using graphic novels to engage incarcerated youth in a variety of authentic writing activities.

CONNECTING GRAPHIC NOVELS TO THE STANDARDS

As mentioned previously, the standards of several national educational associations promote the use of graphic novels with students. The AASL's (2007) *Standards for the 21st-Century Learner* state, "Multiple literacies, including digital, visual, textual, and technological, have now joined information literacy as crucial skills for this century" (p. 3). The following AASL standard specifically addresses visual literacy:

> 2.1.6. Use the writing process, media and visual literacy, and technology skills to create products that express new understandings.

Also, in its *Adolescent Literacy: A Position Statement*, the IRA (2012) lists one of its principles as "Adolescents deserve access to and instruction with multimodal, multiple texts" (p. 7). Finally, the Common Core State Standards (CCSS, 2014) recommend teachers use informational texts in a range of formats, such as graphic novels, to help students meet grade-level standards. The visuals in graphic novels can be an effective way to support the information provided in the accompanying text for readers who fail to meet minimum literacy standards.

WRITING IS NOT APART FROM LIVING

In an article about their study working with expelled Canadian students, Hughes, King, Perkins, and Fuke (2011) state, "Reading and writing graphic novels can be motivating for struggling students and reluctant readers, and can also support development of the multimodal literacy skills needed for school and workplace success in the 21st century" (p. 601). One of the reasons that at-risk students, including incarcerated youth, are motivated to read graphic novels is that many graphic novels represent their own lived experiences. An example of a graphic novel that incarcerated youth can relate to is *Yummy: The Last Days of a Southside Shorty* (Neri, 2010), which tells the true story of Robert Sandifer, an eleven-year-old growing up in a crime-ridden Chicago neighborhood in 1994. An abused child raised by an overwhelmed grandmother, Yummy joined the Black Disciples gang. The nickname "Yummy" came from Sandifer's love of Snickers bars and cookies. He was given a gun and, when aiming at a rival gang's members, he shot and killed a fourteen-year-old neighbor girl who was sitting on her front stoop. At first, other gang members hid and protected Yummy from capture by the police, but they eventually executed him so he could not implicate them. Because Yummy was so young, the story of his short life and death shocked the nation, and his mug shot was on the cover of *Time* magazine in September 1994.

This book does an exceptional job of showing multiple sides of the complex problem of gang violence: the role poverty and his upbringing had on Yummy's choices, why young people join gangs, and the grief felt by all members of the community after the shooting of the innocent teen and Yummy's subsequent death. The graphic novel takes what young adolescents might see as a right-or-wrong issue (gang membership) and shows why the gang was so attractive to Yummy, and how child welfare services failed him.

According to the 2010 National Youth Gang Survey (NYGS), there are approximately 29,400 gangs composed of 756,000 members in 3,500 jurisdictions in the United States (Sickmund & Puzzanchera, 2014, p. 69). Therefore, many of the teens in juvenile justice facilities know all too well the challenges of Yummy's crime-filled world. Yummy's story can serve as a metaphor for their lives, or the lives of those around them. It can help teens reflect on some of their own lived experiences, which can lead to authentic writing experiences. As Bowen (1957) wrote, "Writing, I think, is not apart from living."

Teachers can use *Yummy* as a read-aloud, showing the stark black-and-white illustrations with a document camera. After a group discussion about the book, students can brainstorm possible solutions to the problem of gang violence, and write their own problem-solution essays. This allows students to focus on the topic of gangs and examine different sides of a complex and timely issue. The combination of art and text in *Yummy* makes for ideal writing prompts, and can serve as touchstones for other engaging discussions and writing activities. Some suggested writing prompts for *Yummy* are listed below. Teachers can have students respond to one or more of these prompts, depending on how much time is available for the lesson. These prompts are adapted from the

Teacher's Guide for *Yummy*, located on the Lee & Low website at https://www.leeandlow.com/books/2724/teachers_guide:

- Why do kids join gangs? What motivates Robert "Yummy" Sandifer to join the Black Disciples?
- Do you think Yummy's troubled childhood excuses his behavior? Does his age? Explain.
- Have you or someone you know ever been the victim of a crime? How did it make you, or the person you know, feel? How did you, or the other person, feel about punishing the offender?
- Does Yummy have any redeeming qualities? Use evidence in the book to support your response.
- If Yummy had had a different kind of childhood, do you think he would have been a different person? Explain.
- How do your surroundings, your neighborhood, compare to Roseland, Yummy's neighborhood? How might your neighborhood or surroundings make a difference in your behavior?
- On page 63, Roger wonders if he would have turned out like Yummy if he had grown up like him. What do you think? If Yummy had had a different kind of childhood, do you think he would have been a different person? Explain.
- Why do the Black Disciples end up killing Yummy? What does that tell you about the Black Disciples? Why isn't Yummy expecting this?
- In the introduction to the story, the author says, "I invite you [the reader], to sort through all the opinions . . . and discover your own truth about Yummy." What do you think is the truth about Yummy? Why?

The experience of reading *Yummy* and writing their thoughts about his life can help students reconsider their personal views of gang life and their current lifestyles as incarcerated youth. The process can also help them reflect on decisions they have made in the past, as well as their future goals.

Another graphic novel that is relevant to the lived experiences of incarcerated youth is *Fist, Stick, Knife, Gun: A Personal History of Violence in America* by Geoffrey Canada (1995). This poignant coming-of-age autobiography begins in the South Bronx in 1958. Geoffrey is four years old when his mother first begins to teach him how to avoid being a victim. Geoffrey learns to navigate his sketchy neighborhood through the "sidewalk" boy code of fist, stick, knife, and gun. Reading this powerful autobiography can foster meaningful and creative writing activities with students who can relate to Canada's experiences surviving in a single-parent home in a rough neighborhood.

The publisher, Beacon Press, provides an extensive Teacher's Guide for *Fist, Stick, Knife Gun: A Personal History of Violence in America*, available at http://www.beacon.org/Assets/ClientPages/FistStickKnifeGuntg.aspx. One of the recommended activities is a journal writing assignment, through which students offer their personal reflections about quotes from the book. The assignment directions from the website are provided below, along with some examples of quotes from four of the chapters:

Read each of the following quotes from *Fist, Stick, Knife, Gun* and choose one from each chapter on which to write a journal reflection. Connect the quote to events in the book, to observations made in class discussion, or to events in your life or the lives of the people you know.

Chapter Eighteen
"Did the long tough prison sentence deter people from selling drugs?"

Chapter Nineteen
"This was a block that people who could afford to had long since fled, a block you could find in any city in America."

Chapter Twenty
"We discovered long ago that we cannot save children without making as strong an effort to help their parents."

Chapter Twenty-Three
"But there are things that government could and should do right away to begin to end the violence on our streets."

WORDLESS GRAPHIC NOVELS

Another activity that can inspire students to write is to use wordless graphic novels as a springboard for writing narrative text. Many struggling readers find wordless graphic novels less intimidating than those that include text. Students are able to "read" the pictures to interpret the thoughts and actions of the characters, as well as the story's plot. Students will vary in their predictions about what is coming next in the story, since no two readers will comprehend the story in exactly the same way.

A wordless graphic novel about the contemporary topic of immigration is Shaun Tan's *The Arrival* (2007). Tan's compelling illustrations tell the story of an immigrant leaving his family and traveling to a strange land, where he will build a new life, with new hopes and dreams for himself and his family. The immigrant wrestles with conflicting emotions of leaving his homeland behind, while anxiously anticipating an unpredictable life in a new country. The use of color and visuals in *The Arrival* can help the reader understand the challenges of immigration and assimilation experiences.

Teachers can use *The Arrival* to teach students how to develop a narrative by studying the novel's panels and how they create a sequence of events. Then, students can write narratives based on the graphic novel that describe the setting of the book, develop dialogue, and create descriptive details. Writing prompts, such as the following, can be used by teachers to stimulate their students' writing:

- What are the character's first impressions when he arrives at his new country?
- What are the character's challenges when he finds himself in a strange land?
- What is your favorite illustration in the book, and why?
- What part do color and shading have to do with the story's plot?
- Describe your thoughts about reading a wordless graphic novel. Was this an effective format for the story? Why or why not? (Gavigan, 2014)

Two other wordless graphic novels that can be used for creative writing activities are *Ricardo Delgado's Age of Reptiles Omnibus. Vol. 1* (Delgado, 2011), a dinosaur comic without captions, and *Robot Dreams* (Varon, 2007), a portrayal of enduring friendship between a dog and a robot.

MEMOIRS/PERSONAL NARRATIVES

As part of many writing curricula, students are asked to write a memoir or personal narrative. Graphic novels can be used as an effective first step for this assignment. It can be helpful for students to read graphic memoirs before they begin writing their own personal narratives. Reading and viewing graphic novel memoirs can be less intimidating than reading text-only memoirs for at-risk readers and writers. These novels can help students determine what topics they will write about from their own lives.

The award-winning graphic novel *March: Book One* (Lewis, Aydin, & Powell, 2013) provides a vivid firsthand account of Congressman John Lewis's lifelong struggle for civil and human rights. Based on Lewis's personal story, it also reflects on the highs and lows of the broader civil rights movement. Erin Eddy, an English language arts teacher at Mills Park Middle School in North Carolina, has her students search through the graphic novel for visual and verbal examples of racism, discrimination, and segregation. Then, she asks them to respond to the following writing prompt:

- Why did the author choose to show some of these examples through text, and some through visuals? Discuss the impact of these various forms of communication.

Erin also uses the following prompts to have her students engage in creative writing responses to the graphic novel:

- How do the author and illustrator help the reader distinguish between John Lewis's childhood story line and his present story line?

- Compare and contrast how the authors help us distinguish between words that were sung, spoken, preached, and/or heard over the radio.
- For parts of the story, Powell relays his images against a black background while others are relayed against a white background. Chart when he does each and discuss why this might be. Discuss how page design and backgrounds help communicate the story and its messages.
- Discuss how Powell uses art between pages 60 and 63 to relay the passage of time in Lewis's life and narrative (E. Eddy, personal communication, April 5, 2016).

Two other award-winning graphic novels that can be used to introduce memoir writing activities are *Maus: A Survivor's Tale* (Spiegelman, 1986) and *Stitches: A Memoir* (Small, 2009). With *Maus*, the author-illustrator traces his father's imprisonment in a Nazi concentration camp through a series of disarming and unusual cartoons arranged to tell the story as a novel. *Stitches*, a finalist for the 2009 National Book Award and finalist for two 2010 Will Eisner Comic Industry Awards for the prize-winning children's author, depicts a childhood from hell in this searing yet redemptive graphic memoir.

FROM CONSUMERS TO CREATORS OF GRAPHIC NOVELS

In the previous writing activities, students were largely consumers of graphic novels, reading them before completing writing assignments. Another effective writing activity is to give students the opportunity to be creators of graphic novels, developing their own stories using images and text. Creating comic strips and graphic novels allows struggling writers to practice their written language skills in ways that are not as intimidating as writing essays and papers. Writing the plot and dialogues in a sequential art format can be an engaging process for students. For example, when graphic novelist Mark Crilley worked with students to tell their stories through graphic novels, he found that it helped them realize that "writing is not boring." He also discovered that they learned "the importance of conflict, the use of dialogue to reveal character, and how crucial rewriting is to the writing process" (Crilley, 2009, p. 29).

Teachers can have their students use writing utensils and paper, or comic creation websites, to learn the process for developing plot, characters, dialogue, and setting. The following websites allow students to produce their own comic stories and view the work of their classmates:

Comic Master: http://www.comicmaster.org.uk/
Strip Generator: http://stripgenerator.com/strip/create/
Make Beliefs Comix: http://www.makebeliefscomix.com/Comix/
Pixton: http://www.pixton.com/create

Listed below are two activities that teachers can use to develop writing skills when students create their own comics:

- Have students create a comic strip telling about a positive day in each of their lives, either a positive day from that year, or a day they would like to have. Then, create a wall of comic strips where students can share their work.
- Have students create an instructional comic strip that demonstrates to others how a process should be completed. See HowToons at http://www.howtoons.com/ for examples of this type of comic strip (Moorefield-Lang & Gavigan, 2012).

Students can also work collaboratively to create a graphic novel on authentic topics. For example, incarcerated youth in South Carolina, along with a graphic illustrator, wrote a graphic novel for other teenagers to educate them about HIV/AIDS and to prevent the spread of the disease. The graphic novel, *AIDS in the End Zone* (Albright & Gavigan, 2014), is a fictional story of a high school football player who will do anything to recoup his starting quarterback position, including attempting to get his rival infected with HIV. The students who participated in the *AIDS in the End Zone* project recognized that the process of creating the graphic novel helped them improve their writing skills. As one student stated, "[It] helped us brush up on writing skills because it was a different genre/different way to express yourself." His classmate added, "It is a fun way to develop writing skills while learning about the topic" (Gavigan & Albright, 2015, p. 45).

CONCLUSION

In the words of one teacher, "We need to take advantage of every learning opportunity to engage our students in a way that acknowledges the visual world in which they live" (National Council of Teachers of English, 2008). The sequential art in graphic novels can help incarcerated youth develop writing skills in creative and authentic ways. Whether incarcerated youth are reading graphic novels and writing their reflections about them, collaboratively writing graphic novels about life's challenges, or creating comic strip instructions for their classmates, they are using sequential art in engaging ways that can help them improve their visual literacy and written language skills.

REFERENCES

Albright, K. S., & Gavigan, K. (Eds.). (2014). *AIDS in the end zone*. Columbia: University of South Carolina Press.

American Association of School Librarians (AASL). (2007). *Standards for the 21st-century learner*. Retrieved from http://www.ala.org/aasl/sites/ala.org.aasl/files/content/guidelinesandstandards/learningstandards/AASL_Learning_Standards_2007.pdf

Bowen, C. D. (1957, December). *Atlantic*. Retrieved from http://www.brandyvallance.com/for-writers

Brunner, M. (1993). *Retarding America: The imprisonment of potential*. Portland, OR: Halcyon House.

Canada, G. (1995). *Fist, stick, knife, gun: A personal history of violence in America*. Boston, MA: Beacon Press.

Common Core State Standards (CCSS). (2014, July). *Common Core State Standards Initiative: English language arts standards*. Retrieved from http://www.corestandards.org/ELA-Literacy

Crilley, M. (2009). Getting students to write using comics. *Teacher Librarian, 37*(1), 28–31.

Cummings, M., Bardack, S., & Gonsoulin, S. (2010). (2016, January 10). *Issue brief: The importance of literacy for youth involved in the juvenile justice system*. Washington, DC: The National Evaluation and Technical Assistance Center for the Education of Children and Youth Who Are Neglected, Delinquent, or at Risk. Retrieved from http://www.neglected-delinquent.org/nd/docs/literacy_brief_20100120.pdf

Delgado, R. (2011). *Ricardo Delgado's age of reptiles omnibus. Vol. 1*. Milwaukie, OR: Dark Horse.

Drakeford, W. (2002). The impact of an intensive program to increase the literacy skills of youth confined to juvenile corrections. *Journal of Corrections Education, 53*(4), 139–144.

Foley, R. M. (2001). Academic characteristics of incarcerated youth and correctional educational programs: A literature review. *Journal of Emotional and Behavioral Disorders, 9*(4), 248–259.

Gavigan, K. (2014). Comics make great prompts: Using graphic novels to teach writing in college classrooms. In M. Miller (Ed.), *Class, please open your comics: Essays on teaching with graphic narratives* (pp. 40–51). Jefferson, NC: McFarland Press.

Gavigan, K., & Albright, K. (2015). Writing from behind the fence: Incarcerated youths and a graphic novel on HIV/AIDS. *Journal of Adolescent & Adult Literacy, 59*(1), 41–50.

Hughes, J. M., King, A., Perkins, P., & Fuke, V. (2011). Adolescents and "autographics": Reading and writing coming-of-age graphic novels. *Journal of Adolescent & Adult Literacy, 54*(8), 601–612.

International Reading Association. (2012). *Adolescent literacy: A position statement for the Commission on Adolescent Literacy of the International Reading Association*. Newark, DE: International Reading Association.

Lewis, J., Aydin, A., & Powell, N. (2013). *March: Book one*. Marietta, GA: Top Shelf Productions.

Moorefield-Lang, H., & Gavigan, K. (2012). These aren't your father's funny papers: The new world of digital graphic novels. *Knowledge Quest, 40*(3), 30–35.

National Council of Teachers of English. (2008). Using comics and graphic novels in the classroom. *Comics Chronicle*. Retrieved from http://www.ncte.org/magazine/archives/122031

Neri, G. (2010). *Yummy: The last days of a Southside shorty*. New York, NY: Lee & Low Books.

Sickmund, M., & Puzzanchera, C. (Eds.). (2014). *Juvenile offenders and victims: 2014 national report*. Pittsburgh, PA: National Center for Juvenile Justice.

Small, D. (2009). *Stitches: A memoir*. New York, NY: Norton.

Snyder, H. N., & Sickmund, M. (Eds.). (1999). *Juvenile offenders and victims: 1999 national report*. Washington, DC: Office of Juvenile Justice and Delinquency Prevention.

Spiegelman, A. (1986). *Maus: A survivor's tale*. New York, NY: Pantheon Books.

Tan, S. (2007). *The arrival*. New York, NY: Arthur A. Levine Books.

Varon, S. (2007). *Robot dreams*. New York, NY: First Second.

Weiner, S. (2004). Show don't tell: Graphic novels in the classroom. *English Journal, 94*(2), 114–117.

Chapter Eight

The Places We Can Go

Book Clubs for Social Justice

Jennifer L. Doyle, Elizabeth M. Bemiss, and Mary E. Styslinger

"The more that you read, the more things you will know. The more that you learn, the more places you'll go" (Dr. Seuss, 1978).

As we glance at the paintings with Dr. Seuss quotations written so carefully upon them (see figure 8.1), we reflect on the relationship between reading, theory, and action. What had so easily begun as a six-week study of book clubs with incarcerated students forever changed us. The students we met and grew to appreciate in that very short period of time have remained with us in spirit, though we were not able to remain in contact with them. We have carried them with us just as we carry the painted parting gifts from one office to the next. It is for these students we write this chapter, which introduces why and how to implement book clubs at a juvenile correctional facility.

WHY BOOK CLUBS?

We are teachers from very different backgrounds. One of us taught high school English, another taught elementary school, and the last is now a university professor struggling to transform theory into practice. What we have in common is a commitment to adolescent literacy and social justice. We recognize the potential of teachers to be agents of change through both their content and pedagogy. But we have struggled with the ways and means to promote action beyond our classroom doors. What can we and others do to interrupt the cycle of oppression in the communities that surround us?

We decided to take action and promote some small change in the literacy lives of youth incarcerated not too far from the university where we take and teach classes. We knew there was a positive correlation between increased literacy and decreased recidivism (Brunner, 1993), and we hoped to offer students a literacy experience beyond the traditional tutoring session (Drakeford, 2002). We planned to enable students an opportunity to inquire, interrogate, and challenge inequities and injustices through text. In order to translate social justice theory into practice and address issues of power and privilege through content and pedagogy, we wanted to foster literacy experiences centered on collaborative talk.

We talk to make sense of ourselves, others, ideas, and the world that surrounds us. Clearly, talk advances understanding. Applebee, Langer, Nystrand, and Gamoran (2003) determined dialogic approaches to literacy instruction have a strong effect on improving students' comprehension of literature. And Gilles (2010) has made clear the connection between critical thinking and talk, encouraging us to probe deeper into texts and build ideas with others through dialogue. Talk that occurs around a book can be invaluable to students' civic education as they hear and honor differing opinions and perspectives. As Dewey (cited in Moyers, 1992) reminds, the habits of democracy include the ability to "grasp the point of view of another, expand the

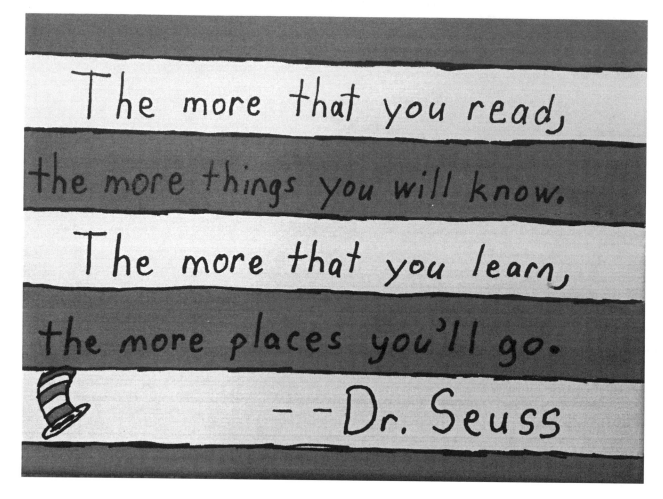

Figure 8.1.   Painted Dr. Seuss quotation presented by student. *Doyle, Bemiss, and Styslinger, chapter authors.*

boundaries of understanding, [and] debate the alternate purposes that might be pursued." Talk enhances our understanding not only of text, but of each other and the world.

Book clubs offer an ideal forum for talk. Made up of a small group of readers who meet on a regular basis, club participants engage in systematic discussion about books and/or other texts of the members' choice, and use a variety of open-ended response methods to prompt discussion. Membership in book clubs varies and can involve the presence of a teacher or volunteer (O'Donnell-Allen, 2006).

In accordance with social justice theory, book clubs have the potential to challenge traditional content and pedagogical practices. As groups self-select a book, participants have the opportunity to read texts more culturally congruent with their own understandings of the world. More culturally responsive text may allow students to learn life lessons as they see themselves and their circumstances reflected in the reading. Such texts may encourage students to explore ways of dealing with day-to-day issues and problems, examine political and social issues, and gain cultural insight and knowledge (Fredricks, 2012).

This is particularly important for incarcerated youth because it creates a possibility for critical discourse. Critical book clubs relate texts to members' historical, cultural, and social issues, providing a means to discuss social and cultural identities and offering insight into readers' theories on race, gender, and behavior (Fredricks, 2012; Park, 2012), making them a perfect vehicle for reclaiming voice, altering power dynamics, and creating spaces for students to learn routes for advocacy on issues important to them.

BOOK CLUBS FOR SOCIAL JUSTICE

Using a social justice theory framework, we facilitated a book club at a nearby JDC (juvenile detention center). We responded to the call from Thein, Guise, and Sloan (2011) for the implementation of a more teacher led approach to book clubs for students to examine texts critically, hoping this intersection of literature and activism could guide us to "read both the word and the world" (Freire & Macedo, 1987). Literature holds the power to create diverse and engaging pedagogy, while providing dialogic spaces for students to reflect upon their beliefs and philosophies. We consider it our responsibility to expose students to issues surrounding social justice within texts and encourage educators to develop a critical manner of observation while reading. We are committed to pedagogical practices that allow students the opportunity for critical discourse around culturally responsive text. Through book club discussions that recognize and analyze issues of power, we hoped to guide students to deeper understandings of selves, others, and realities. Beyond that, however, we hoped to create our book club as a call to action—a way for students to engage in social justice even from behind the fence.

In this book club, we also drew upon critical race theory (CRT) to examine the students' experiential knowledge and cultural resources (Delgado Bernal & Villalpando, 2002) as a way to promote social justice. CRT recognizes the intersectionality and compounding jeopardies of race, racism, and power with other forms of oppression such as sexism, classism, or sexual orientation (Bell, 1992; Delgado, 1989). CRT informs our social, cultural, and constructivist approaches to understanding because we believe knowledge construction is generated within greater social and cultural milieu, where experiences, beliefs, and relationships with others are driven by context, culture, and social interactions through multiple ways of being in the world (Ramsey, 2004; Rogoff, 2003).

The purpose of our book club was to combat stereotypes and oppression in the everyday lives of students who are incarcerated. We wanted to build students' literacy skills while fostering critical collective action and promoting practical decision-making skills. Our hope was for students to develop voice and agency to promote critical collective action within their school and their communities outside the JDC. We wanted to transform book clubs into a program of social change and collective action through critical race pedagogy as a way to promote social justice.

HOW WE FACILITATED BOOK CLUBS FOR SOCIAL JUSTICE

We began our book club experience by asking for volunteers from the population of students at the JDC. This was facilitated by an on-site coordinator. Any and all students who were interested in a book club were welcome to join; we ended up with four males in our book club. We began our initial meeting with an icebreaker, followed by a reading interview. We asked questions about their interests in school, what types of assignments they enjoyed and disliked in English class, what types of books they enjoyed reading, and what their general interests were. In addition, we acknowledged ourselves as individuals and readers during the interview process. This reciprocal process built community and trust with students—both of which are key elements to developing a successful book club with incarcerated youth.

Using the information gathered from the interviews, we presented various high-interest young adult novels to students, briefly spoke about each one almost as a sales pitch, and then conducted a book pass with each novel. We placed one novel on each chair in the circle (*Monster* by Walter Dean Myers, *Muchacho* by Louanne Johnson, *Bad Boy: A Memoir* by Walter Dean Myers, *The Absolutely True Diary of a Part-Time Indian* by Sherman Alexie, and *Lockdown* by Walter Dean Myers). We set a timer and gave ourselves one minute to peruse and rate the novel before we had to "pass" it to the next person. We then allowed students to vote on their favorite novel. Our group, made up of sixteen- and seventeen-year-old African American males in grades nine through eleven, chose to read *The Absolutely True Diary of a Part-Time Indian* (Alexie, 2007).

Once students selected the novel, we provided them with reading calendars. Each calendar had the dates for our book club, and the students chose the amount of pages to be read by each meeting. Student choice was important, allowing them agency over their book club experience. The students also created their own list of expectations for themselves, their classmates, and for us as facilitators. Again, this provided the students agency. Students emphasized "respect for classmates," "respect for women in the room" (Jen and Elizabeth, the facilitators), "open-mindedness," and the avoidance of "profanity."

Throughout remaining meetings, we used the novel as well as additional media to teach students the tenets of CRT—such as the permanence of race and racism in society, the challenge to dominant ideology, the legitimization of experiential knowledge of people of color, and the commitment to social justice—through comedy video clips, music videos, and handouts. These curricular choices encouraged student-led discussion on both race in relation to the chosen novel and in relation to our students' lived experiences and the pursuit of social justice. Through writing invitations, exit slips, and discussion we helped the youth develop ways in which they could promote social justice not only within the confines of incarceration, but also within their communities back home.

Our students welcomed the opportunity to speak about issues of social and racial justice as it related to both the book and their own lives. Using the literature as a starting point, many students connected to and opened up about their own experiences with racism in schools as well as within the criminal justice system. One youth shared how he noticed when he went to court that "all the colored people went to jail . . . and you could see the segregation." His peers were then able to build upon those shared experiences and brainstorm ways in which they could change their own worlds by sharing their experiences with youth in their communities and creating programs to help the elderly. Another student shared that the one thing he wanted to change in his community back home was "the way young people look at things," and how he was going to do this by reaching out to the youth in his community. All of our students often spoke of wanting to make the world a better place for the future generations; one particular student shared in our final meeting his resolve for this, revealing that he had a daughter of his own back home.

These conversations, however, could not have occurred without careful planning and community building throughout. We began each book club with writing invitations (see the appendix) that deliberately asked students to connect their reading to life experiences. We also answered the writing invitations with the students and shared our own personal experiences. It was important to us that the students knew they were the ones in charge of the book club and that we were there to learn with them rather than talk at them. We were at once both facilitators and members of the book club. Discussions of race, racism, power, and privilege cannot occur without mutual trust and respect, and this mutual trust and respect cannot be developed without also making ourselves vulnerable. We remained cognizant of all of this as we planned and facilitated book clubs.

CHALLENGING THE STATUS QUO THROUGH BOOK CLUBS

Throughout this book club experience, our students positioned themselves as self-empowered individuals who recognized the impact of incarceration on their own lives, as well as the lives of those around them, and sought to accomplish individual and communal goals beyond the walls of the JDC. In addition, there was a clear dichotomy among our students' reader identities and those informed by institutions, such as school. All the students voiced positive opinions about reading, stating that it "makes you more wise," "gives you something to think about," and how "a book gives you somewhere to go when you don't have nowhere to go." However, many of the students voiced their displeasure for traditional reading in schools and expressed the ways in which teachers and other school staff had the ability to "make or break" them in their paths to incarceration as they discussed a part in the novel where the main character, Junior, was dismissed by a teacher due to his race. One student shared how "there always was that one teacher that tried, you know, to keep me down," and the other students connected to this as well in their personal experiences with school and teachers.

Students recognized power structures in society, distinguishing among power inequities in various institutions such as school and the criminal justice system, and examined how these differences impacted their daily lives. They often spoke of the endemic and systemic inequities and an awareness of institutionalized racism and systemic ways of functioning in society, yet they held on to a belief in meritocracy as a form of self-empowerment. As one youth shared, "Man, anyone can have a better future, you feel me? They just gotta put their minds to it." Indeed, this need for hopefulness and a belief in meritocracy is vital when working with any group of students, but particularly incarcerated students. While students were able to identify particular examples of the myriad of inequities created and perpetuated in society, they were also able to identify specific ways in which they could address some of these problems within their communities, which was essential to promoting social justice and agency among our students. Throughout this book club with incarcerated youth, we found our students developed voice and agency through literacy in a place that limited both. As one student stated, the book club experience "helped me think clear . . . and taught me to express myself by being a better reader."

LESSONS LEARNED FROM OUR BOOK CLUB

While we celebrated some successes in our book club experience, we still struggled to turn theory into practice. We knew Thein et al. (2011) had noted the limitations of personal response for meeting the goals of a critical multicultural pedagogy as some students may not feel comfortable sharing in a group. And we discovered firsthand the challenges of teaching about race, racism, power, privilege, and CRT as white women with students of color. We learned that reading, writing, analyzing, and critiquing existing literature and having ongoing discussions and critical reflection aids in the process. A balance needs to be drawn between racial realism and optimism so students see hope for a better future and that we all have a responsibility to work toward that better future.

Moreover, we reflected on the ways in which white researchers cannot be authoritatively antiracist (Thompson, 2003) in a way that centers whiteness in the fight for racial and social justice. Throughout the study, we consistently reflected and discussed the ways in which we had to be cautious not to play the role of the "good white" or the "white savior." We had to be reflective, cautious, and deliberate about how to prevent misinterpretation, misinformation, and misrepresentation of people of color that could ultimately allow racism to persist.

We do not claim to have proceeded through this process perfectly. Reflexivity and constant decentering of whiteness is a recursive and ongoing process that takes honest, often harsh critiques of personal actions and their consequences. We urge others who undertake such research to continue to be reflective, cautious, and deliberate in their continued work for social and racial justice as well.

For students who are incarcerated, participation in book clubs provides an opportunity for them to construct a metaphorical, as well as physical, third space in which to expand and extend knowledge and allow for freedom and growth. Furthermore, participation in book clubs gives students space to be heard by peers and the outside world. Students develop voice through book clubs and a sense of agency over their reading, as well as their lived experiences.

For teachers, it is important to note that student choice is an integral part of students developing their identities as readers. Talk and dialogue are central to agency and ownership over reading. In addition, our book club with incarcerated youth proved to be a valuable tool for extending student knowledge and construction of identity. Incorporating social justice and critical race pedagogy into book club discussions can lead students from awareness toward action when promoting social justice in their lives and their communities. Teachers need to humanize their students and allow themselves to be human as well, reciprocally sharing knowledge and constantly building a community of learners in which the students hold valuable knowledge as well as the teacher. While we realize this is a process that takes time, it is a fundamental aspect of developing book clubs that promote critical thinking, agency, and social justice.

As we once again glance at the Dr. Seuss paintings, we wonder if these students realize how much they taught us. During book clubs, we learned to interrogate not just literature but subsequently theory, practice, and the complex and complicated relationship between the two. Their talk guided us to challenge the status quo in text, in society, in readers, in teachers, in ourselves. Through reading and talking in book clubs, the "more things" we all came to know.

APPENDIX: WRITING INVITATIONS

1. List ten things about yourself that we would know if we "really knew" you.

2. Write down three statements about yourself. Two of them will be truthful and one will be a lie. We will guess which one is the lie.

3. If you had to pick a "theme song" for your life, what song would you pick and why? What does this song tell us about your life?

4. Please read the following statements and circle the term that best describes how much you agree or disagree with each one (Strongly Disagree, Disagree, Agree, Strongly Agree). Use the space below each statement to explain why you selected your choice for each statement.

    a. An individual's race plays a determining factor in his or her future.
    b. Race is a determining factor in hopefulness of a better future.
    c. Different races get better or worse treatment accordingly.
    d. All people get treated equally, regardless of their race or ethnic background.
    e. In order to gain access to success in our society, one has to give up his or her cultural identity.

5. What can you learn from Junior about life and how to overcome struggles?

6. How can you work toward racial and social justice outside of these book clubs?

7. What is one thing you want to change in your community back home? This can be big or small. How are YOU personally going to make that change happen?

REFERENCES

Alexie, S. (2007). *The absolutely true diary of a part-time Indian.* New York, NY: Little, Brown.

Applebee, A. N., Langer, J. A., Nystrand, M., & Gamoran, A. (2003). Discussion-based approaches to developing understanding: Classroom instruction and student performance in middle and high school English. *American Educational Research Journal, 40,* 685–730.

Bell, D. (1992). *Faces at the bottom of the well.* New York, NY: Basic Books.

Brunner, M. S. (1993). *Reduced recidivism and increased employment opportunity through research-based reading instruction.* Washington, DC: Department of Justice, Office of Juvenile Justice and Delinquency Prevention.

Delgado, R. (1989). Storytelling for oppositionists and others: A plea for narrative. *Michigan Law Review, 87,* 2411–2441.

Delgado Bernal, D., & Villalpando, O. (2002). An apartheid of knowledge in academia: The struggle over the "legitimate" knowledge of faculty of color. *Equity and Excellence in Education, 35*(2), 169–180.

Drakeford, W. (2002). The impact of intensive program to increase the literacy skills of youth confined to juvenile corrections. *Journal of Correctional Education, 53*(4), 139–144.

Fredricks, L. (2012). The benefits and challenges of culturally responsive EFL critical literature circles. *Journal of Adolescent & Adult Literacy, 55*(6), 494–504.

Freire, P., & Macedo, D. (1987). *Literacy: Reading the word and the world.* Westport, CT: Bergin & Garvey.

Gilles, C. (2010). Making the most of talk. *Voices from the Middle, 18*(2), 9–15.

Moyers, B. (1992, March 22). Old news and the new civil war. *New York Times,* Editorial.

O'Donnell-Allen, C. (2006). *The book club companion: Fostering strategic readers in the secondary classroom.* Portsmouth, NH: Heinemann.

Park, J. Y. (2012). A different kind of reading instruction: Using visualizing to bridge reading comprehension and critical literacy. *Journal of Adolescent & Adult Literacy, 55*(7), 629–640.

Ramsey, P. G. (2004). *Teaching and learning in a diverse world: Multicultural education for young children.* New York, NY: Teachers College Press.

Rogoff, B. (2003). *The cultural nature of human development.* New York: Oxford University Press.

Seuss, Dr. (1978). *I can read with my eyes shut.* New York: Random House for Young Readers.

Thein, A. H., Guise, M., & Sloan, D. L. (2011). Problematizing literature circles as forums for discussion of multicultural and political texts. *Journal of Adolescent & Adult Literacy, 55*(1), 15–24.

Thompson, A. (2003). Tiffany, friend of people of color: White investments in antiracism. *Qualitative Studies in Education, 16*(1), 7–29.

Part III

Inspiring Partnerships

Chapter Nine

Theme for English B

Teaching and Learning with Incarcerated Youth

Peter Williamson, Megan Mercurio, and Constance Walker

"Sounds like shoes crackling over gravel and dry oak leaves skittering down the street in the wind; smells like smoky sausage on a skillet wafting out of the greasy restaurant window overhead." —Lamont, incarcerated student

Crouching next to his desk, I am pressing Lamont to generate more descriptive words for his narrative. I am struck by his keen focus on keeping his writing true to the events he is describing. He resists embellishment. Uniformed and in many ways locked into the classroom where we are working, Lamont believes that as a writer he must combat the urge to romanticize his life outside the juvenile detention center; he must convey his experiences with precision and accuracy, or they won't be real. Lamont and I have discussed the liberty in writing that the artist, the poet, the storyteller enjoy, but he sees his priority as telling it like it was. The gravel was more like hot cinder, and there were no leaves. He describes a dusty racetrack with no runners on it. Lamont is sprinting, leaving. He has to get away fast or he will be trapped, surrounded.

A glance around the room confirms that these conversations are happening elsewhere in clusters. The lead teachers are each kneeling next to other students' desks, and one teacher is telling the other to make sure that she has a chance to read Juan's newest work before he saves it to the server and puts his laptop away. The other adults in the room—these are my students who are teacher candidates in an urban teacher residency program— are scattered around the room trying to determine the best body posture, the right tone, the most accessible way to enter into coaching conversations with youth they have only just met. The teacher candidates are nervous about interacting with inmates, but the candidates are quickly realizing that these young people are eager to talk about their work. What allows these relationships to be built so quickly? I think about the likelihood that the youth in this classroom have had fewer opportunities to really engage with teachers about their work. They don't really see themselves as students; school has not served them so far.

Though I have been in this classroom many dozens of times, I am still making sense of the ways its physical and social composition—its bricks and mortar, both physical and emotional—seem predictable and contradictory at the same time. The cinder block walls are covered with posters of leaders and thinkers like Maya Angelou and Che Guevara, but the doors are magnetically sealed and the windows are bulletproof glass. The teachers are dressed professionally but casually, and the guards are uniformed and carrying walkie-talkies that spew a constant stream of crackling information that is deeply disconnected to what is happening in the classroom. The classroom is filled with laptops and Smart Boards and lights for growing plants in the dark, but the students can't hold pencils longer than four inches, and they must return these to a bucket when they leave each day; pencils can become weapons in the wards where students live, and they can become tools for suicide in the cells where students sleep. The teacher's desk at the front of the room is raucously crowded with a collection of twenty Beanie Babies representing every sort of real and imagined animal, but the stuff of childhood is totally absent everywhere else. This is not a place for toys, and the youth who live here vehemently deny any affiliation with anything childlike. Rows of uniformed teenage inmates are facing rows of stuffed animals dominating a desk that has been transformed into a stage.

Our work with the student inmates in the school within San Francisco's Juvenile Justice Center is filled with contradictions. Some of them are obvious, even to the students. For example, we teachers put learning at the center of everything that we do, but that is not why the students are here. Some of the contradictions are less obvious, though they all require deep analysis and reflection. For example, many of the students in our classes don't see themselves as students when they are in the outside world, but here they come to see themselves as voracious readers and accomplished writers with powerful stories to tell. Further, as teachers we strive to create safe learning environments where all students can learn, and while our work is aligned with the overall aims of the Learning Center, this goal seems antithetical to goals and the organization of the authoritarian institution where our school is set. Classroom community and collaborative learning environments—hallmarks of good teaching in the schools we aim for our teachers to create—are structurally at odds with the norms and purposes of a detention center. This means that authority is also distributed differently here, given that guards and other staff populate every classroom, and the teachers are necessarily less a part of the authority structure in the classroom. How does this reposition the role of the teacher in establishing and maintaining relationships with students?

Over the course of our collaboration for the past seven years, we have come to think of these contradictions as the paradoxes of our work. They are tensions between truths that coexist because our pedagogical purposes and motivations are necessarily at odds with those of the system and, to some extent, the students we serve. While we have written elsewhere about some of the daily curricular challenges that we face as teachers and teacher educators working inside the juvenile justice system (Williamson, Mercurio, & Walker, 2013), in this chapter we extend our discussion of how the paradoxes of our work afford particular teaching opportunities as well as provide a framework for what new teachers can learn from observing practice in this setting.

Though we all come from long histories of teaching English, we are also an interdisciplinary group of educators who are collaborating to unpack and improve our practice for multiple purposes and audiences. Megan Mercurio is an English teacher who is National Board certified and has been teaching at the Learning Center for ten years. While completing her credential at San Francisco State University, Megan started volunteering as a meditation teacher at the San Francisco County Jail. This experience led her to accept her first full-time teaching job at the Learning Center. Constance Walker is a special education teacher who is also National Board certified. After completing her credentials at San Francisco State University, she began working as a special education teacher for students with emotional and learning disabilities. She has now been teaching at the Learning Center for eighteen years and has been collaborating with Megan for eight. Peter Williamson was an English and special education teacher for many years before becoming a teacher educator in 2006. A founder of the San Francisco Teacher Residency program and now the faculty director of the Stanford Teacher Education Program for secondary teachers, he began collaborating with Megan and Constance as a way to explore what new teachers can learn from classrooms that are deeply focused on serving students who have struggled at the edges of our school systems and society. For several years, Peter has been facilitating clinical instructional rounds at the Learning Center for new teachers, where they participate in guided observations with Peter and then have opportunities to debrief what they have seen with Megan and Constance (Williamson & Hodder, 2015).

In this chapter, we weave together our three voices to describe and unpack the many paradoxes that form the core of our work. Our purpose is to provide a teacher-centered discussion of pedagogical considerations for curricula and strategies that can be effective with incarcerated youth. The chapter begins with a discussion of teaching behind bars, where the roles of teachers and students are recast through a prism of institutionalized authority. We conclude with an exploration of what new teachers can learn about the promises and pitfalls of practice in these settings, and what teacher educators can do to help prepare professionals to be successful working with incarcerated youth.

A PARADOX OF PLACE AND LEARNING ENVIRONMENTS

When Megan and Constance began teaching, the school was in a building that echoed all the characteristics of a jail. Students were isolated at nearly all times in housing units. They were rarely permitted to leave the units or interact with inmates from other wards. Teachers moved in and out of the five housing units to teach classes as if they were guests. Perhaps unsurprisingly, the learning environment was punctuated with anger and violence. The task of creating a classroom community apart from the jail culture felt nearly impossible. As teachers, we felt like daily visitors in someone's unruly and sometimes terrifying house: students confined to their rooms banged on doors while guards squawked at each other through walkie-talkies, adding to the confusion. Mice scurried in and out of the bathrooms. We felt powerless to overcome chaos.

The move into the new $50 million Juvenile Justice Center changed the way both teachers and students viewed the possibilities for educating and transforming young people who are incarcerated. Given a new building with unfamiliar design, both apprehensions and hopes about the changes that would come preoccupied the adults who would be working inside. We wondered how the youth would respond to attending school in the new Education Center down the hall from the housing units. In one radical change, the *entire* population (except the maximum-security unit) would be present, simultaneously, in the Education Center. Staff who would be supervising the young people as they moved from their units to the classrooms and back worried about potential rioting. While teachers despised the awful conditions in the old building, we were also nervous about what lay ahead.

We did not anticipate the sense of renewal that the new facility would inspire in both the teachers and even the students. The gray bricks on its exterior concealed what we soon came to see as a hidden sanctuary of learning. Our school, architecturally fashioned in a circular shape, allows students to move from classroom to classroom through a series of connecting doors. In addition to its seven academic classrooms, it came stocked with a public library, a full-time librarian, and indoor-outdoor gymnasium. Because we were given almost complete autonomy to create our own classroom atmosphere and curricula, we designed the English classroom to be aesthetically and energetically antithetical to the jail. We created a space that celebrates diversity with the hope of inspiring students to reimagine themselves as academics capable of lifelong learning.

Our new classroom, a colorful and more peaceful environment, depicts not only social justice heroes from all cultures, but also student essays, poems, and work from visiting community artists and activists. Though time with our students is limited, we aim to provide the best possible educational experience in a resource-rich classroom. After moving to the new Justice Center, we discovered that environment matters tremendously. Moving the school into its own space transformed the context. More than ever before, the school is now the center of the students' day, and the institution's administration considers the school day the highest priority. The positive attitudinal shifts among the various players has brought significant change, helping to refocus the school's as well as the institution's mission as restorative rather than punitive.

Yet as we accumulate more resources and continue to improve our facility and our practice, we cannot help but see the paradox in our approach. Our school is a place of incarceration and, sadly, the beginning of a path that will end in prison for some of our students. This raises questions for us as educators, who also believe that our goal is to prepare students for the world where they live. Should we focus our efforts on creating the most inspiring educational experience possible in the hope that extensive access to both support and materials for positive progress will lead to a decrease in recidivism? Or will the relative abundance of the new environment allow youth to become comfortable with the institution and, as a consequence, will this comfort level diminish their fear of recidivism and bind them to the prison industrial complex even more deeply?

A student once told us that we should try to get a beanbag chair for the classroom. We said we would do our best to obtain it. Then, after thinking more about his request, he said, "Actually, you shouldn't get it. You shouldn't have the rug, or the fancy chairs, or the computers. Kids get comfortable here, and then they don't mind it anymore."

With that statement this student named one of our deepest fears; he identified one of the paradoxes of creating safe creative learning environments in classrooms that are also jails. While we want the students to become successful, engaged youth who come to see themselves as scholars rather than outcasts of the public education system, we do not want them to become comfortable with—or dependent upon—the institution that confines them. In a building filled with guards, magnetically locked doors, and an authoritarian approach to everything regarding social interaction and order, students frequently acknowledge that they feel safer and more able to focus on the inside than they do on the outside. Can this paradoxical relationship between incarceration and safety—between access to resources inside and the relative lack of access outside—lead to recidivism? We are always sad when we have to say farewell to students who are leaving our facility to reenter society or transfer to a different sort of rehabilitation program, though we also hope that the change they experience will be good for them in the long run. In important ways, we hope that we will never see them again. We are devastated when we see them return, sometimes cheerfully calling out to us, "I'm back!" as if they are returning home to some familiar place. Their return can only mean failure for us.

Lessons about Place and Learning Environments for Novice Teachers

Through instructional rounds, novice teachers can observe the classroom contexts at the Learning Center while they also experience ways that inmates engage the curriculum and the materials that are available to them. Key questions focusing these guided observations include: How does the classroom environment seem to shape how students interact with the material, the teachers, and each other? How does the classroom environment relate to our own images of what it might mean to attend school in jail?

During our briefing sessions before entering the classrooms, we discuss both our predications and expectations about what we will "see" and how it might impact our thinking as teachers. Peter reminds the novice teachers that from a sociocultural perspective people and places are mutually constitutive (Casey, 1993), and understanding the connections between the places students are confined and how they can act on their surroundings can help educators know more about how student identities are formed in contexts like jails. Theorists like David Gruenewald remind us of the importance of "place conscious" education (2003a, 2003b), arguing that places are "profoundly pedagogical" in that they play a deep role in how we learn about and experience the world. For educators in jails, place-conscious preparation may help students develop tools for looking beyond the "danger of a single story" (Adichie, 2009) narrative that frames incarceration as an unbreakable cycle of recidivism. It can also provide educators with frameworks for examining how some spaces are explained away through terms like "inner city" and "urban blight" (Hollins, 2012; Milner, 2012). Novice teachers visiting the Learning Center can come to see jail as a space for growth and possibility, a paradox that can have implications for how they structure their own future classrooms and work to engage students who seem disconnected from the enterprise of school.

In a sense, witnessing the paradox that is at play in the classrooms inside the jail is part of the pedagogical purpose of structured observations through clinical rounds with novice teachers. We want the teachers to expand their understanding of the relationship between learning context and student identity, witnessing for themselves the ways students respond to having access to rich learning environments even when many of them have had less access to those resources historically.

Students are often eager to start writing and reluctant to stop at the end of a period. When asked to read what they have written, they frequently jump at the chance to share their words with their peers. Sometimes at the end of a period the challenge for teachers seems to be more about helping students transition away from working on their own writing so they can leave rather than motivating them to finish their work. What the novice teachers witness is an eagerness among students to produce and share that belies the popular view that students who end up in places like this are unmotivated and unskilled. The students in this jail are beginning to see themselves as scholars, at least while they are here.

A PARADOX OF IDENTITIES

In a powerful account of a school visit where the purpose was to see how a district was implementing new social services for supporting low-income students from historically underserved communities, Pedro Noguera tells the story of an assistant principal who casually points out a boy of eight or nine and says, "Do you see that boy? There's a prison cell in San Quentin waiting for him." When pressed, the principal explains that many members of the child's family are already in prison. "I can see from how he behaves already that it is only a matter of time before he ends up there, too," says the principal (Noguera, 2003, p. 341).

Decades of unexamined assumptions about who gets in trouble and how schools should respond have led to the "zero tolerance" and other punitive policies that many claim are partially responsible for the school-to-prison pipeline and the overrepresentation of youth of color in jails (Cuellar & Markowitz, 2015; Skiba, 2000). Disrupting the school-to-prison pipeline will involve, among other things, a concerted effort on the part of teachers and teacher educators to reframe the conversation about what behavior means and how educators can see students as people with needs rather than as problems to be removed or contained. In response to the administrator that Noguera encountered during his visit, he asked, "Given what you know about [the student], what is the school doing to prevent him from going to prison?" (Noguera, 2003, p. 341). Noguera's question resonates across the infrastructure of our public education system. What can we be doing as a profession to challenge the unexamined assumptions that are the currency of our school disciplinary and youth corrections systems?

Our strategy has been to invite people—new teachers, administrators, politicians—into our classrooms so that they can witness the humanity and vitality of our students. Visitors often realize that their negative preconceptions about incarcerated youth are overgeneralized and deeply informed by biased popular representations of young people of color. Marc Lamont Hill (2013) has argued that "anti-baggy pants legislation, civil injunctions against gangs, and imposition of juvenile curfews represent a few of the ways we have created a political and cultural environment that reframes youth as social burdens rather than sites of investment, love, protection, or hope" (p. 7).

Though visitors to our classroom generally come away reporting that their perspective has shifted to seeing incarcerated youth as children rather than something more onerous or dangerous, the paradox at play is that the youth are both children and adults at the same time. It is undeniable that our students live complicated lives that are filled with adult strains and responsibilities, often much more so than students from more privileged backgrounds. These students have been witnesses to, victims of, and sometimes perpetrators of violence. They have had to find the means, often at early ages, to find money to feed themselves, their families, and their friends. The pressure of these burdens has caused many of them to become hypervigilant, angry, and depressed. They find ways to mask their vulnerabilities, and these strategies often seem like behaviors associated with overt bravado, defiance, or "shutting down." They have learned to hide behind the mask of appearing to be unreachable, uncaring, and impenetrable thugs. They know they are often perceived as being older than they are.

Sometimes this façade erodes in unexpected ways. For example, we created a prominent display of Beanie Babies—tiny stuffed animals that span a realism continuum from giraffes to dragons—on the desk at the front of our room. We don't say much about them, and students rarely question their presence. But without prompting, some students inevitably ask if they can have Beanie Babies sit with them on their desks during class. As improbable as it seems, the students will carefully position the stuffed animals so that the Beanie Babies become a part of their work environment—next to their laptop or above their writing—and the toys seem to keep watch over the students while they work. Often, this action seems to make it okay for more of the class to ask for animals of their own, and we often see a Beanie Baby at nearly every desk (or on students' shoulders or heads). Students who have been with us longer have their favorites. The students' appreciation of the Beanie Babies has been a compelling reminder that they are still children in need of comfort, protection, and hope.

We believe that these simple symbols of innocence provide some comfort and solace to students who are under duress. Perhaps the toys calm the fears and loneliness that are triggered by being away from home, and perhaps they mitigate some of the anxieties that these imprisoned young people feel about the future. For example, it was poignant when one student, Terrance, returned from court visibly upset after being sentenced to two years at an out-of-state institution. He walked into class, quietly sidled up to the front desk, and grabbed the zebra he lovingly referred to as "his little homie." He positioned the stuffed animal on his desk and stroked his neck and belly throughout the remainder of class.

Allowing students to be children and human in the midst of a system that is organized to correct and confine them may allow them to learn something about maintaining their own humanity after they have left. So often, they enter the system having already rejected it. Rather than reinforce institutional norms that seek to control and regulate the students, we strive to amplify their voices by rewarding their participation and encouraging them to read their work publicly (sometimes with a microphone) and express themselves openly within a supportive environment. We are surprised when even the most hesitant students are persuaded to share their writing once they know it will be safe. There are many ways that we try to foreground what we understand to be opportunities to acknowledge the childhoods that they are missing by being here. A former student told us privately that juvenile hall is the only place where kids can be their true selves, unmasked.

Lessons about Identity and Students' Projected Selves for Novice Teachers

By observing in settings like the Learning Center, novice teachers can interrogate their assumptions about students who seem resistant to "doing school." They can also question what motivates behaviors that are difficult to interpret in the rush of daily classroom practice. For most of us, it is too easy to conclude that students who seem disengaged or who appear to be actively resistant or defiant will end up being rejected by the system because that is what they, the students, want. From that perspective, their destiny is failure, at least when it comes to school. But like the administrator who sentenced the eight- or nine-year-old boy to San Quentin, we might also conclude that those students are just headed for prison anyway and there is little that teachers can do to change this fate.

Describing teachers who resist adopting deficit views of students who struggle—particularly in high-need, urban environments—Etta Hollins (2012) urges us to prepare teachers who can learn to "swim upstream" against the current of low expectations in schools by sustaining visions of hope and possibility in the face of difficulty. The instructional rounds at the center are oriented toward helping novice teachers develop a deeper understanding of where "those students" go when they disappear from their general education classrooms for weeks or months. Problematizing the assumption that students are cutting class or taking extended family trips, observations help novice teachers see a different view of how students act and interact in settings that are organized to provide different kinds of support. Key questions focusing these guided observations include: How do students represent their ideas and lived experiences, and how do the identities they present align with popular beliefs about students in jail? What pedagogical strategies work with students who struggle at the fringe of schools and society?

Once during instructional rounds—toward the end of the observation of the English class—a teacher candidate nervously approached Peter with a question. She believed that she recognized one of the young men in the class, and she wondered if it would be okay to talk with him. She and the student had been actively avoiding acknowledging each other throughout the visit, but she believed that he was the student who had mysteriously disappeared from her algebra class about three weeks earlier. With no word from anyone about where he had gone, the teacher had assumed that he was either cutting class or visiting Mexico with his family; students sometimes took long and unexpected trips without telling anyone where they were going. Now she realized that he was being detained. Could she acknowledge that she recognized him? Could she talk with him about what was happening with him?

When she approached him, smiling, he seemed to melt: his teacher recognized him, cared about him, wanted to talk with him, saw him in this place. Though she had only been his student teacher for some months before he was arrested, the fact that someone from the outside cared enough to acknowledge him transformed his whole person: he beamed a teary smile, and he eagerly spoke with her about what he was missing in school. Someone recognized him for somebody other than who he was in jail.

Helping novice teachers understand the systems that both support and confine our youth can help them develop deeper understandings about what students experience and how systems work to disenfranchise youth even while they are trying to protect and reform them. In this case, the teacher learned that her assumptions about students and their motivations and actions deserved further interrogation. And everyone participating in rounds that day learned something about the complex identities that students necessarily construct in order to survive the systems they encounter as they negotiate the world around them.

DISCUSSION

By framing our practice as teachers and teacher educators working with youth in the juvenile justice system as a set of paradoxes, we are able to highlight the myriad ways that teaching and learning in this space offers us opportunities to explore how the relational and curricular aspects of our work can inform practice beyond the walls of the jail where we teach.

It is possible to help youth find relevance in, and take ownership over, the school-based content even when they don't see themselves as students and they may have given up on "doing school" altogether. Finding their voice can help students see themselves as readers and writers, and they are eager to be heard when they believe that someone is listening. We wish that they could take their pencils back to their wards so that they could write into the night.

It is possible for people who have experienced and perhaps have perpetuated trauma to also be children, and allowing them to experience childhood can be part of the restorative practice of preparing them for what comes next. As educators, we have the ability to create the conditions for students to express their true selves—even those they believe they should hide. Behavior always means something, and teachers can establish a practice of inquiring into what students are communicating through the various masks they wear.

It is possible for teachers to combat deficit views of students and the communities where they live, even in places like jails. Disrupting the school-to-prison pipeline will require educators everywhere to examine the assumptions that we make about the skills, motivations, and experiences of students who struggle at the fringe of our schools and society. Observing students learning in jail can help teachers question their beliefs about what "those kids" can do and what they believe is important.

Further, teachers can come to understand the larger systems that are in place to support and confine our youth. Understanding what students experience when they have been removed from our classrooms is an important part of understanding how to relate with them when they return. Teachers have an opportunity to help students make sense of the various worlds they traverse, and teachers are uniquely positioned to help them process their experiences through self-expression and self-reflection.

Many of our students have attended multiple schools from which they have been suspended, expelled, or otherwise excluded from whatever counts as meaningful participation in those settings. Some have been sent directly from school to juvenile hall. We know these students are capable individuals, and we want their voices and needs to be reflected and projected beyond our walls. As Mike Rose (1989) reminds teachers in *Lives on the Boundary*, "Students will float to the mark you set." In jails, this mark is too often set tragically low, and students are "bobbing in pretty shallow water" (p. 26). We argue that this is true, in part, because the expectations for teachers in these contexts are pretty low as well, and that part of our collective work is to hold ourselves accountable for raising this mark. Disrupting the school-to-prison pipeline will require teaching and learning to be both transformed and transformational, and for educators and students alike to believe that this is possible.

REFERENCES

Adichie, C. N. A. (Producer). (2009). *The danger of a single story* [TED Talk]. Retrieved from http://www.ted.com/talks/chimamanda_adichie_the_danger_of_a_single_story

Casey, E. (1993). *Getting back into place: Toward a renewed understanding of the place-world.* Bloomington: University of Indiana Press.

Cuellar, A. E., & Markowitz, S. (2015). School suspension and the school-to-prison pipeline. *International Review of Law and Economics, 43,* 98–106.

Gruenewald, D. A. (2003a). The best of both worlds: A critical pedagogy of place. *Educational Researcher, 32*(4), 3–12.

Gruenewald, D. A. (2003b). Foundations of place: A multidisciplinary framework for place-conscious education. *American Educational Research Journal, 40*(3), 619–654.

Hill, M. L. (2013). Teaching in the age of incarceration. *English Journal, 102*(4), 16–18.

Hollins, E. (2012). *Learning to teach in urban schools: The transition from preparation to practice.* New York, NY: Routledge.

Milner, R. H. (2012). But what is urban education? *Urban Education, 47*(3), 556–561.

Noguera, P. (2003). Schools, prisons, and social implications of punishment: Rethinking disciplinary practices. *Theory into Practice, 42*(4), 341–350.

Rose, M. (1989). *Lives on the boundary: A moving account of the struggles and achievements of America's educationally underprepared.* New York: Penguin Books.

Skiba, R. J. (2000). When is disporportionality discrimination? The overrepresentation of black students in school suspension. In W. Ayers, B. Dorhn, & R. Ayers (Eds.), *Zero tolerance: Resisting the drive for punishment in our schools.* New York: New Press.

Williamson, P., & Hodder, L. (2015). Unpacking practice with clinical instructional rounds in the San Francisco Teacher Residency program. *International Journal of Educational Research, 73,* 53–64.

Williamson, P., Mercurio, M., & Walker, C. (2013). Songs of the caged birds: Literacy and learning with incarcerated youth. *English Journal, 102*(2), 31–37.

Chapter Ten

Reading Buddies

A School-University Partnership

Mary E. Styslinger and Timothy R. Bunch

"An incarcerated young person is black, white and every shade in between. He is talkative and quiet. He reads and doesn't read. Some are beyond proficient, and some are still working readers. . . . They've made crucial mistakes, but so have we." —Charles, English teacher candidate

"Teachers are with us, not against us." —Stanley, incarcerated student

When we sit back at the end of a too quick summer semester and read through reflections written by our students, we realize the power of this partnership in creating change in attitudes and perspectives. We are two English teachers, colleagues who know each other from past experiences with the National Writing Project, who teach very different learners in very different spaces. One of us is a university professor, preparing future English teachers; the other is a classroom teacher, teaching English and so much more to incarcerated teens. One of us teaches at a state university; the other teaches at the state Department of Juvenile Justice (DJJ). While the teaching contexts may differ, our philosophies are quite similar. Committed to teaching for social change, we advocate for culturally and socially relevant curriculum and instruction that promotes equity and empathy with regard to issues of race, class, ability, language, religion, sexuality, and gender.

Commitment to these social justice beliefs has led to a long-term exchange of ideas. We have sustained and motivated each other through years marked by professional challenges including decreases to budgets and increases in standards. Always asked to do more with less, we have tried to figure out ways to grow our students' thinking around personal, societal, cultural, and world issues through reading. We have wanted them to recognize who they are, who others are, and who they can be. During one conversation a few years back, we both expressed a desire to move students beyond their current modes of thinking and realm of experience. We agreed that our students needed more encounters with others in order to foster greater sensitivity to issues of diversity, which we hoped would expand learning in our classrooms. A solution seemed obvious. We would bring our learners together in a collaborative, literacy-related partnership. Eight years later, we are still reading buddies behind the fence.

This chapter begins with our reasons for engaging in this kind of partnership. Next, we explain what we do to support student and teacher literacy learning. The chapter concludes with a summary of what we have learned as a result of bringing new teachers together with incarcerated youth.

WHY DO WE DO THIS?

Broaden Perceptions of Self and Others

Our reasons for entering into this collaboration are many. First and foremost, we want to broaden current perceptions held in relation to self and others. We do this to help future teachers and DJJ students outgrow beliefs about who they and others are as teachers and readers.

For example, most of us become English teachers because we love literature. As brand-new teachers, we imagine ourselves inspiring students with *The Great Gatsby* and *Hamlet*. How many of us become English teachers because we want to teach reading? When we bring our students together, teacher candidates begin to envision themselves as teachers of literacy as well as literature. Through this collaborative endeavor, teachers come to understand the daily expectations and responsibilities of supporting readers. They administer assessments and plan for strategic teaching, recognizing and guiding the individual meaning-making process. Making literacy decisions challenges teacher candidates to trust in their abilities and recognize limitations. While their given purpose is to help students gain confidence as readers, they simultaneously gain confidence as literacy teachers.

Along with expanding their perceptions of the teacher-self, this experience can prompt teacher candidates to reconsider perceptions they hold of others. In the hopes of providing more culturally and socially responsive teaching preparation, we provide this opportunity to collaborate with students who are, more times than not, academically, culturally, ethnically, and/or socioeconomically different from themselves. We know the teaching population does not mirror the population of our nation's diverse student body. According to a presentation by the National Collaborative on Diversity in the Teaching Force (2004), 60 percent of public school students in 2001 were white, 17 percent black, 17 percent Hispanic, and 4 percent Asian/Pacific Islander; however, 90 percent of America's public school teachers were white, 6 percent black, and less than 5 percent identified themselves as being a member of another race. Acknowledging this reality is an important first step. Researchers have argued for quite some time that teacher education programs need to move beyond traditional coursework and include field experiences that allow teacher candidates to work with culturally diverse students in culturally diverse settings (Adams, Bondy, & Kuhel, 2005; Causey, Thomas, & Armento, 2000; Cooper, 2007; Keengwe, 2010; Sleeter, 2001; Vaughan, 2005).

However, it is important to make clear that difference does not denote deficiency. Through this partnership, English teacher candidates discover the literacy(ies) and possibility inherent in each student, seeing beyond the label of *incarcerated* or *at-risk* youth. They come to realize presumptions are not always correct—stereotypes not always valid. Experiences such as these are invaluable in teacher education programs because, as Cooper (2007) has indicated, they can encourage a change in conceptions and dispositions about students and their diverse backgrounds.

DJJ students shift their understandings of self and others as well through this experience. As teacher candidates interview DJJ students about their literacy backgrounds and interests, the students come to realize that what they say matters to a teacher. When teacher candidates provide choices of text based solely on what they have come to learn about their interests, students become aware that someone is closely listening. What they say is significant. Their words and actions define and drive the curriculum. While we don't want to romanticize the potential of this literacy partnership, we do believe that if an individual student feels more significant, then he or she is more likely to recognize the significance of others.

DJJ students come to recognize themselves as instructors and readers, as part of the education process for a prospective teacher. They educate us about books and strategies. Whereas many of the DJJ students have had adverse experiences with schooling (one student in particular was incarcerated for threatening to blow up a school), they enter into a literacy partnership with a teacher candidate. As a result, they come to know how teachers listen, plan, facilitate, and reflect around reading, gaining a new perspective on and appreciation for others.

Foster Metacognition on Reading and Life

Another reason for engaging in this kind of collaboration is the potential for greater metacognition among future teachers and DJJ students. Flavell (1976) foundationally referred to metacognition as the process of thinking about thinking. We want English teachers and DJJ students to read, teach, and act metacognitively to analyze experiences and, consequently, learn from them.

Understanding metacognition is imperative for future teachers working with a range of readers who need access to direct and explicit instruction in metacognitive strategies. Metacognitive strategies are self-monitoring and self-regulating behaviors that focus on the processes and products of reading, including readers' awareness of whether or not they comprehend or their knowledge of when and how to employ specific cognitive strategies (Pressley & Harris, 2006). Cognitive strategies are mental and behavioral activities used to increase the likelihood of comprehending, which may include rereading, activating background knowledge, or adjusting reading speed (Van Den Brock & Kremer, 2000).

Conley (2008) suggests that cognitive strategy instruction holds great promise for improving adolescents' reading, writing, and thinking as cognitive strategies foster meaning making through constructive interactions with texts. Comprehension-oriented cognitive strategies include activating relevant prior knowledge and using prediction, generating questions during reading, constructing mental images representing the meanings in texts, summarizing and clarifying the meanings in texts, and analyzing the structural components of narrative and informational texts (Pressley, 2006).

With DJJ students, teachers describe what proficient readers do to understand text and explicitly model those strategies during authentic literacy experiences. We teach comprehension-oriented cognitive strategies such as questioning, inferring, predicting, connecting, summarizing, visualizing, and analyzing structural components. Such strategies help readers become more conscious of the kinds of thinking utilized when reading text.

While we foster metacognition among teacher and student readers, we hope for a sort of transference. As we think more about our reading processes, we can become more metacognitive about other life decisions and subsequent actions. The students at DJJ are incarcerated for a variety of crimes ranging from theft to murder with sentences ranging from six months to six years. The crimes committed originated with a thought that led to a belief that produced an action that resulted in consequences. We maintain that practiced metacognition has the potential to shift beliefs and, thus, actions. Moore and Aspegren (2001) discovered the potential for empowering an at-risk youth reader through reflective reading conversations, and the retrospective nature of this approach may empower learners to make more responsible choices in literacy and life. As DJJ students stop to question the text, will they next time stop to question an action? Will teacher candidates stop to question a method? As DJJ students connect with texts, will they next time connect with others? Will teacher candidates connect with students? As students and teachers think through their reading together, they may become more metacognitive in other situations.

Enhance Literacy Teaching and Learning

A final reason for this collaborative literacy endeavor is our desire to enhance literacy teaching and learning. As educators, we hope this partnership deepens student understandings of teaching and reading.

Whereas the teacher candidates at our local state university possess undergraduate degrees in English and enroll in graduate coursework, pursuing master's degrees in teaching leading to initial state certification, they have no prior experience planning, facilitating, or assessing learning experiences specifically in reading. This university-school partnership provides the needed opportunity to meet professional standards related to literacy in an authentic way. English teacher candidates are able to translate new learning around reading theory and research into actual practice. They are able to administer assessments and plan for teaching, supporting the individual reading and meaning-making process.

DJJ students can enhance their learning through increased literacy exposure and experience. The need for improved literacy instruction in juvenile correctional facilities has been widely documented by researchers (Brunner, 1993; Christle & Yell, 2008; Krezmien & Mulcahy, 2008; Vacca, 2008). Also recognized is the potential that reading interventions offer for juvenile correctional facilities. Christle and Yell (2008), Vacca

(2008), and Brunner (1993) have noted that literacy efforts can reduce youth incarceration, decrease recidivism rates, and create reading gains.

WHAT DO WE DO?

So what is it that we do? Because we want to broaden perceptions, foster metacognition, and enhance literacy teaching and learning, we bring university and incarcerated students together each summer. The experience is required for secondary English teacher candidates enrolled in a course designed to develop high school teachers' knowledge and understanding of the linguistic, psychological, and social foundations of reading instruction. Participation in this partnership is voluntary for DJJ students.

Before meeting with middle and high school students, English teacher candidates first develop their foundation for teaching literacy through reading, talking, and writing with colleagues. They reflect on prior literacy experiences, explore definitions of reading, become familiar with readers who struggle, and foster a more critical perspective. Along with reading professional texts related to research, theory, culture, and pedagogy, teacher candidates immerse themselves in young adult and urban literature, knowing they need to select novels to read alongside students and wanting to expand their text knowledge. After literacy and literary groundwork is established, teacher candidates read and learn with DJJ students over a three-week period. Students are partnered randomly on the first day and then meet with this same student, on average, every other day. DJJ students, all male at this particular facility, range in age from twelve to eighteen years with reading levels from fourth grade to college level. All meetings with students are held at the correctional facility, but some teacher planning occurs in a university classroom.

At the initial meeting, following a group icebreaker, student-partners come to know each other. Teacher candidates have been forewarned not to ask any questions related to why the student is here, and instead ask questions about school, sports, music, and the usual likes/dislikes in an effort to find books of interest for the student. Teachers share information about their own likes/dislikes as well. Eventually teacher candidates administer and record a reading interview (Goodman, Watson, & Burke, 2005) adapted for adolescent readers. This interview format helps teachers discover how students define reading and consider the role it plays in their lives. Responses to the questions provide insight into the literacy background, environment, and experiences of students.

After this first meeting, teacher candidates listen to the recording a number of times and take detailed notes, thinking about this reader. What makes him unique? How did he come to language and reading? What are his interests? Instead of deficits, what "funds of knowledge" does he bring to literacy? Teacher candidates summarize their thinking in relation to this student and justify their book selections.

At the second meeting, teacher candidates talk with students about what they have learned from the interview and share their notes, modeling their academic efforts and asking any necessary follow-up questions. Eventually they introduce book choices, explaining each and allowing students to select among two or three recommended novels. Once a novel is selected, they collaboratively establish a reading calendar.

Over the next meetings, teacher candidates front-load, support, and extend the reading processes of students, planning and facilitating prereading, during reading, and postreading strategies in relation to the novels selected (see textbox 10.1).

Novels selected to read by incarcerated youth.

The Hunger Games	Suzanne Collins
Eye of Minds	James Dashner
*Forged by Fire	Sharon Draper
Among the Hidden	Margaret Peterson Haddix
Savage Hulk	Marvel
Monster	Walter Dean Myers

Slam	Walter Dean Myers
Sunrise over Fallujah	Walter Dean Myers
Cat & Mouse	James Patterson
Nevermore: A Maximum Ride Novel	James Patterson
The Angel Experiment: A Maximum Ride Novel	James Patterson
Private Down Under	James Patterson and Michael White
The Boy in the Black Suit	Jason Reynolds
All American Boys	Jason Reynolds and Brendan Kiely
Harmony House	Nic Sheff
Uglies	Scott Westerfield

*Two students chose to read this novel.

In addition, teacher candidates administer and record a miscue analysis including a retelling in order to better understand the cue systems (graphophonic, syntactic, and semantic) utilized by individual readers. A miscue analysis is a diagnostic tool developed by Goodman (1969) that provides teachers a window into an individual reader's processes, assessing students' comprehension based on samples of oral reading. At a meeting following the administration of the miscue analysis, teacher candidates facilitate a retrospective miscue analysis (RMA) designed to foster metacognition. During an RMA, teacher candidates lead students to consider reading miscues through guided questioning. Teachers select miscues for discussion and help students become more reflective about their own reading processes, asking questions (Goodman & Marek, 1996) such as: Does the miscue make sense? Does the miscue sound like language? Was the miscue corrected? Should it have been? Does the miscue look like what was on the page? Does the miscue sound like what was on the page? Why do you think you made this miscue? Did that miscue affect your understanding of the text? After each meeting, students in both contexts reflect on experiences through writing and consider what they are learning about reading, readers, teachers, teaching, and each other.

WHAT HAVE WE LEARNED?

As mentioned, we engage in this collaboration to broaden perceptions, foster metacognition, and enhance literacy teaching and learning. But we have to wonder if we are accomplishing these objectives. What is gained from bringing together new teachers with incarcerated youth? As we return to reading through the written reflections, we realize more about what DJJ students and teacher candidates are learning from this experience.

Reading Is about Meaning

Throughout the collaboration, students at DJJ discover and reiterate that reading is more about the process of meaning making and less about reading words. They indicate that reading is "more than what's on the page." You have to "think about what you are reading" and you "gotta think outside the box." Students recognize that "sometimes you have to read between the lines and actually try to figure out what it is the writer [is] really talking about." Reading is a process through which to gain knowledge, and more than a few students realize they read too quickly and need to slow down in order to better understand.

Teacher candidates also acknowledge the importance of reading as meaning making, learning how to recognize the difference between reading at a word level and at a meaning level. More so, they come to value teaching reading as opposed to teaching about the text: "Teaching themes, characters, and elements of plot are of little relevance if a student is unable to first comprehend." "By teaching them *how*," a candidate explains, "I am giving them strategies they can apply to whatever else they encounter."

Reading Is an Active Process

DJJ students recognize that in order to understand, a reader has to be a practicing participant in the process. Reading is an active process that requires work to understand. As one student details, "A real reader will question, evaluate, predict, and respond to the material he reads." Another recalls his own process and proficiency: "When we went back and went over my miscues, I saw that I will also read in my own words and put some of my own meanings into the book instead of just reading word for word. . . . I am a better reader then [*sic*] I thought I was."

DJJ students realize their responsibility in becoming more literate, acknowledging they need to find their "likes and dislikes" in order to locate books and genre(s) of interest. A few also declare that reading is a lifelong process, and even proficient readers can improve their reading strategies.

Because they are such proficient readers, teacher candidates are not initially aware of their own meaning-making strategies and admit to having to learn to make the unconscious conscious. Once they discover that reading is not a passive activity, teacher candidates claim "comprehension is a process, not a product," one that is continuously evolving, needing guidance and feedback.

Reading Relates to Life

DJJ students connect reading to experience, conveying that "reading can make you look at things in much more detail." Students make personal connections: "If you pay attention to what you're reading, some situations in the book can relate to the situation in your life." One student even goes so far as to acknowledge, "This experience has taught me not to hide what has happened in the past, but to reflect and elaborate on paper about them." As a result, teacher candidates come to realize the importance of connecting text to student experience and interest. As one candidate summarizes, "Literature can only be 'read' if the reader, himself, has an investment in it."

Teachers and Readers Are Individuals

This collaborative endeavor helps students recognize and value the individual teacher. As DJJ students summarize: "All teachers are not the same," "Some teachers take the time to understand you," and "Teachers have their own unique and genuine style." They come to realize "teachers don't plan to make a subject lame" and many are "concerned about us" and are "dedicated."

University teachers initially harbor reservations about and bias against incarcerated youth: "Despite my best intentions, I had poor expectations of whatever student I would be assigned. I imagined a belligerent boy with a low reading level. What I later saw was an enthusiastic reader who loved to discuss the events of his latest book. This makes it even clearer to me that I must assay each student accurately, longitudinally, and compassionately." Through this experience, teacher candidates come to value the distinctiveness of each reader, realizing that "each reader is unique because of his or her abilities, beliefs, and experiences." We must see beyond a label. The background of readers becomes paramount: "To assume that every student gains access to written language in the same way is to disrespect the uniqueness of each learner." As a result, teacher candidates realize the importance of knowing individual students: "Without at least a partial understanding of the particular interests, dislikes, I have no ability to design a curriculum that will be most effective for him as a learner." Lesson planning must be student centered, and teachers need to collect data on student interests, comprehension, environments, and experiences in order to meet the individual needs of readers. They have to "help each reader based on their individual strengths and challenges and not by 'one cookie cutter formula.'"

Teaching Is Hard Work

And last, students and candidates become more aware of the hard work involved in teaching. University and DJJ students realize the preparation involved, gaining insight into daily planning and instruction. As one DJJ student admits, "Teachers go through a lot of hard work to prepare things for us." Teacher candidates learn to be "organized," but more than this, they come to learn that "everything does not always go to plan. In fact, nothing does." They begin to "go with the flow" and "drop, punt, kick" as students are absent for various reasons including court dates, psych appointments, lockups, speaking engagements, and GED testing. They learn to be flexible and realize there isn't always a "right" way to do things. As one teacher candidate describes, "Teaching needs to be fluid, something that changes shape when it confronts different obstacles." Teachers also grasp the nonstop nature of teaching: "I am in a sprint and I don't really have a definite end in sight."

So do students gather from this collaborative experience what we hoped? Perceptions of self and others are certainly broadened as candidates see themselves as active readers and literacy teachers while recognizing DJJ students as individual and capable readers. Everyone's increased understanding of the work involved in teaching, a result of metacognition, shifts perceptions as well. DJJ students broaden their perceptions of teachers and selves, seeing competence and possibility in both. As students and candidates consider reading as an active and meaning-making process, they deepen their understanding of literacy and teaching. Their reflection on processes including (mis)cue use and comprehension strategies, along with relating reading to life experiences, is additional evidence of metacognition.

Of course there are challenges along the way. Student absences, scheduling difficulties, uncooperative spirits, and time constraints to name a few, but we agree the potential of a partnership between a university and a school—among future teachers and incarcerated youth—should prevail over any difficulty. We can teach for change in literacy and perspective, knowing students will walk away with greater understanding of reading and each other. There is much to be gained from reading behind the fence.

REFERENCES

Adams, A., Bondy, E., & Kuhel, K. (2005). Preservice teacher learning in an unfamiliar setting. *Teacher Education Quarterly, 32*(2), 41–62.

Brunner, M. S. (1993). *Reduced recidivism and increased employment opportunity through research-based reading instruction.* Washington, DC: Department of Justice, Office of Juvenile Justice and Delinquency Prevention.

Causey, V. E., Thomas, C. D., & Armento, B. J. (2000). Cultural diversity is basically a foreign term to me: The challenges of diversity for preservice teacher education. *Teaching and Teacher Education, 16*, 33–45.

Christle, C. A., & Yell, M. L. (2008). Preventing youth incarceration through reading remediation: Issues and solutions. *Reading & Writing Quarterly, 24*, 148–176.

Conley, M. W. (2008). Cognitive strategy instruction for adolescents: What we know about the promise, what we don't know about the potential. *Harvard Educational Review, 78*(1), 84–106.

Cooper, J. E. (2007). Strengthening the case for community-based learning in teacher education. *Journal of Teacher Education, 58*(3), 1–11.

Flavell, J. H. (1976). Metacognitive aspects of problem solving. In L. B. Resnick (Ed.), *The nature of intelligence* (pp. 231–235). Hillsdale, NJ: Erlbaum.

Goodman, K. (1969). Analysis of oral reading miscues: Applied psycholinguistics. In F. Gollasch (Ed.), *Language and literacy: The selected writings of Kenneth Goodman* (pp. 123–134). Boston, MA: Routledge & Kegan Paul.

Goodman, Y., & Marek, A. (1996). *Retrospective miscue analysis.* Katonah, NY: Richard C. Owen.

Goodman, Y., Watson, D., & Burke, C. (2005). *Reading miscue inventory: Alternative procedures.* Katonah, NY: Richard C. Owen.

Keengwe, J. (2010). Fostering cross cultural competence in preservice teachers through multicultural education experiences. *Early Childhood Education Journal, 38*, 197–204.

Krezmien, M. P., & Mulcahy, C. A. (2008). Literacy and delinquency: Current status of reading interventions with detained and incarcerated youth. *Reading & Writing Quarterly, 24*, 219–238.

Moore, R. A., & Aspegren, C. M. (2001). Reflective conversations between two learners: Retrospective miscue analysis. *Journal of Adolescent & Adult Literacy, 44*(6), 492–503.

National Collaborative on Diversity in the Teaching Force. (2004). *Assessment of diversity in America's teaching force.* Washington, DC: National Education Association.

Pressley, M. (2006). *Reading instruction that works: The case for balanced teaching.* New York, NY: Guilford.

Pressley, M., & Harris, K. (2006). Cognitive strategies instruction: From basic research to classroom instruction. In P. Alexander & P. Wine (Eds.), *Handbook of educational psychology* (pp. 265–286). Mahwah, NJ: Erlbaum.

Sleeter, C. E. (2001). Preparing teachers for culturally diverse schools: Research and the overwhelming presence of whiteness. *Journal of Teacher Education, 52*(2), 94–106.

Vacca, J. S. (2008). Crime can be prevented if schools teach juvenile offenders to read. *Children and Youth Services Review, 30*, 1055–1062.

Van Den Brock, P., & Kremer, K. (2000). The mind in action: What it means to comprehend during reading. In B. Taylor, M. Graves, & P. Van Den Brock (Eds.), *Reading for meaning: Fostering comprehension in the middle grades* (pp. 1–31). New York, NY: Teachers College Press.

Vaughan, W. (2005). Educating for diversity, social responsibility and action: Preservice teachers engage in immersion experiences. *Journal of Cultural Diversity, 12*(1), 26–30.

Chapter Eleven

Building Bridges across the Disciplines

Professional Development behind the Fence

Victoria A. Oglan and Janie R. Goodman

"I worry that the reading gap is so deep that the bridge that I offer is too short to reach the other side." —Susan, teacher of incarcerated youth

Imagine driving down a busy four-lane highway and turning onto a long, straight roadway that divides a large, grassy field. You drive slowly forward until you see a large stop sign; a small brick guardhouse; and an imposing, razor-wire-topped fence. Watch as a guard approaches your car window and asks to check your credentials. The tall, electric gate in front of you opens inch by inch. Slowly drive past the gate and hear a loud, metallic clanking sound as the gate locks behind you. Welcome to the Department of Juvenile Justice (DJJ), or the world that many simply call "behind the fence."

We are two former middle and high school teachers with a combined sixty-three years of classroom experience. Currently, we both teach graduate and undergraduate courses in content-area literacy at a large state university. As veteran classroom teachers, we are often called upon to provide professional development for in-service teachers across our state. The landscape of education in the twenty-first century is changing, and all teachers, regardless of teaching positions or situations, are challenged to keep current with new standards, increased technology, certification requirements, and an awareness of current instructional methods that support all learners. Our goal as professional development providers is to support teachers in their efforts to address these changes. This is the story of how we ended up behind the fence and our experiences working alongside the dedicated teachers who devote themselves daily to educating adjudicated juveniles. We use the term "adjudicated" since there is a wide variety of adolescents at different stages of evaluation and/or incarceration within the juvenile justice system. We begin this chapter with a description of the professional development we provided, including background and context for the model. Next, we share what we learned as a result of our experiences behind the fence. We conclude this chapter by sharing the experiences of teachers and possible next steps for continuing professional development.

HOW WE GOT HERE

Our university has long fostered a partnership with the DJJ—a partnership that supports both students and educators. One factor that initially contributed to our work with DJJ is our interest and expertise in disciplinary literacy at the middle and high school levels. The university courses we teach are always in high demand since many states require teachers to have a course in content literacy as part of their certification requirements. A second factor is the trend in education for all content teachers to have a clear understanding of the literacy demands in their disciplines. As a result of these factors, DJJ contacted our university and requested professional development for their educators.

DJJ educators represent a wide range of content areas and disciplines. In addition to teachers of the core disciplines of English, math, science, and history, there are also a variety of career and technology education teachers who teach in skilled trade/technical/life skills/vocational content areas such as horticulture, graphic communications, culinary arts, parenting education, personal finance, accounting, digital desktop publishing, brick masonry, keyboarding, carpentry, and welding. Additionally, professional development sessions often include media specialists, guidance counselors, and special education teachers. Most of these teachers have expert content knowledge but limited pedagogical knowledge in literacy. As a result, the DJJ administrative team felt there was a high need for professional development that would offer this unique mix of educators support in addressing the literacy educational needs of adjudicated juveniles across all these content areas and disciplines.

The educators at DJJ wanted to learn ways to improve their praxis as DJJ students tend to represent a broad range of proficient to struggling learners. In an effort to meet the diverse needs of students, DJJ educators needed professional development that provided effective content-area-differentiated literacy instruction. While current educational research supports strengthening content-area reading strategy instruction for students in middle and high schools (Daniels, 2011; Gallagher, 2004), it is especially true for the students at DJJ—students who may have little or no confidence in their abilities to learn, may lack the motivation to learn, or may face learning challenges (Wexler, Pyle, Flower, Williams, & Cole, 2014). For educators to be equipped to help all students achieve sufficient literacy skills across content areas and disciplines, they need to use their unique content and literacy knowledge to foster students' abilities to read, write, think, and communicate in all disciplines.

PLANNING PROFESSIONAL DEVELOPMENT FOR DIVERSE POPULATIONS

As veteran classroom teachers, we have spent many hours in professional development that was either ineffective or irrelevant. As a result, we have developed a set of beliefs over time that inform our work with teachers. We approached our DJJ colleagues with the beliefs that professional development must:

- be interactive and allow opportunities for professional conversation;
- provide practical, easy-to-implement literacy strategies;
- offer ideas for resources and materials for diverse learners; and
- promote the practice of teachers as reflective practitioners.

Because the teachers who work within the DJJ system have diverse teaching situations, they also have diverse professional needs. The administrative personnel wanted to engage all teachers in the professional development initiative so we e-mailed teachers, asking them for a list of topics for professional development, and received a solid response. The major topics they requested included the following:

- Specific strategy instruction for improving reading and writing in all content areas
- Ways to incorporate the reading/writing workshop model into their instruction
- Methods for improving students' critical and higher-order thinking skills
- Steps to build and foster a sense of community among their learners
- Methods for more effective assessment and evaluation of student learning

As a result of our ongoing conversations with the DJJ administrative personnel, and with input from the teachers, we initially offered three professional development sessions, as shown in table 11.1. All DJJ educators were required to attend these all-day sessions. We provided interactive demonstrations of best-practice teaching ideas that teachers could readily implement into their instruction. These ideas were applicable across all content areas and disciplines.

At the end of the three professional development sessions, teachers consistently remarked that they were encouraged to try the many instructional ideas we shared with them. They also commented that the sessions

Table 11.1.   Department of Juvenile Justice professional development sequence.

Session	Topic	Overview of Goals
1	Writing to Learn as Higher-Order Thinking	Help teachers: 1. broaden their understanding of balanced literacy and the connections between reading and writing. 2. understand the importance of having students make connections between school and the world. 3. offer a variety of differentiated instructional ideas that would foster higher-order thinking in students.
2	Reflecting on Instructional Practice as Critical Thinking	Help teachers: 1. understand that reflecting on practice needs to be ongoing and daily. 2. recognize the connections between reflection as critical thinking and improved practice. 3. understand that reflection is the genesis of professional development.
3	Helping Disenfranchised Learners Celebrate Success as Readers and Writers	Help teachers: 1. understand the importance of establishing a classroom community where all learners are valued as readers, writers, and thinkers. 2. recognize the many challenges textbooks present to students because of their structure and complexity. 3. understand that building student confidence may improve student competence.

provided them with many opportunities to reflect on their beliefs and practices and make efforts to change things that were not working in their classrooms.

An unexpected result for us occurred when we provided teachers with multiple opportunities to read, write, converse, collaborate, and think both independently and in small groups. One of the things they commented on was how much they enjoyed being grouped with teachers from all content areas. They enjoyed the professional conversations, and they made new friends along the way. They also realized the benefit of sharing ideas as a professional learning community and commented how much they wanted to continue the learning journey. They said they felt more confident in their ability to assess their students as readers and writers and to use their new instructional practices to engage their students in learning. They said they were better equipped to help their students and felt they had tools to help them build a thinking classroom where students have multiple opportunities to celebrate success as readers, writers, and thinkers.

OUR LEARNING CURVE

As veteran providers of professional development, we recognized that we had a rich opportunity to learn with and from the teachers at DJJ. Even though we were in an unfamiliar physical environment, we discovered both differences and similarities between the professional experiences of the teachers at DJJ and our professional experiences as public school teachers.

Differences for DJJ Teachers

The DJJ teachers shared through conversations and written reflections how their teaching lives differed from what we had experienced as public school educators. Some of the major differences included:

- a teaching contract of 235 days;
- year-round school;
- fluid and transitory population of youthful offenders;
- single-gender/multiage classes;
- restricted environment that limits planning, teaching methodology, use of technology, access to resources, and parental contact;
- completion of all work in class with no assignments outside class;
- correctional officers assigned to all classrooms and hallways; and
- a feeling of being invisible to the profession at large.

Similarities for DJJ Teachers

At the core of every effective teacher is the belief of caring about and making a difference in the life of a student. As we spent time with the DJJ teachers, we came to understand how much they, like all effective educators, cared about their students and wanted them to succeed both inside the classroom and outside the fence.

Teachers shared with us how they worked to create in their classrooms what Noddings (2005) has called the "ethic of care." They held high expectations for their students and described for us the ways in which they affirmed their students' efforts to learn. DJJ teachers took pride in the accomplishments of their students, choosing to view them through the positive lens of what they could do in the future rather than the deficit perspective (Bourdieu, 1986; Nieto & Bode, 2012) of what they had done in the past.

Over time, we learned how DJJ teachers seemed to feel a sense of duty and obligation to create close and trusting relationships with their young, vulnerable students. They collectively believed education was the best way to alter the trajectories of their students' lives. Teachers let us know that helping them improve their instructional practices provided them with new ways to help their students envision successful lives. Once again, in written reflections, they expressed their feelings about teaching adjudicated juveniles by writing:

- I dream that all the students will be able to leave with life lessons.
- I want my students to succeed.
- I try to see the best in each student.
- I show them that it's okay to want more for themselves.
- I am driven to help students make better choices in their lives.
- I want to be able to help my students learn and grow as young adults.

Moving Beyond Our Learning Curve

This professional development experience with the DJJ educators turned out to be a learning opportunity for all of us. We discovered how, despite the differences faced by the teachers at DJJ, they have found ways not only to survive but to thrive in a challenging teaching situation. Like all effective educators, they are not limited by their circumstances but actively seek opportunities to grow in their professional practices.

TEACHERS' STORIES FROM THEIR PROFESSIONAL DEVELOPMENT EXPERIENCES

One of the most effective methods we had for learning about whether or not the professional development was making a difference in the day-to-day work of the DJJ teachers was through talking with them and listening to classroom stories. By having a small peek inside their classrooms through the stories they told us, we could vicariously witness their successes and struggles with students. Hakim (2007) wrote, "Stories tell us who we are and where we've been" (p. 4). These teachers' stories told us who they were as teachers and what new literacy methods they were willing to try in order to help their students succeed both in the classroom and in life.

Dave's Story (a Pseudonym)

Dave, a former social worker, was a teacher in one of the DJJ evaluation centers where juveniles have residential, court-ordered evaluations prior to the disposition of their judicial case. According to the South Carolina Department of Juvenile Justice (2016), the length of stay in the evaluation center cannot exceed forty-five days. Dave expressed his frustration with this system that he described as a "revolving door" with juveniles coming into the evaluation center for the maximum forty-five days, leaving, getting into trouble again, and then returning for another forty-five days. He said it made his teaching very difficult to organize and plan because students were continuously coming and going from his classes.

In addition, Dave thought the most challenging thing about teaching within the DJJ was "inspiring kids who have no motivation to learn." What compelled Dave to work with these students was "seeing kids who have never experienced success feel proud of themselves." The topic of confidence building competence in learners in the third session prompted Dave to make a significant connection between teaching and learning. He realized that when he built in opportunities for his students to be successful this bolstered their confidence as learners. As a result, this increased their motivation to learn. Dave came to understand that celebrating small successes along the way is a powerful motivator for disenfranchised readers and writers.

Throughout the professional development experience, Dave was an enthusiastic participant, willing and eager to learn new methods to try with his students. Even though he was very experienced with planning reading instruction centered around novels, he admitted this had become problematic based on the transitory nature of the juvenile evaluation system. He felt he was unable to maintain the continuity he wanted for his students to have the chance to read an entire novel.

What made a difference for Dave in the third session was learning about research studies (Brozo, 2002; Herz & Gallo, 1996) supporting the enthusiasm adolescent boys have for nonfiction and informational texts. Because Dave worked exclusively with male students at the evaluation center, he decided to gather as many resources as he could and take them into his classroom for the boys to read.

Dave shared a success he had as a result of the professional development experience. In a written reflection, he wrote, "By providing more informational texts than novels, my students are reading more and understanding the content better." However, he also wrote that one of his challenges was "finding material for every learner at every level." For Dave, pairing his reading instruction with short pieces of authentic nonfiction and informational texts allowed him to create instructional units that worked better with the forty-five-day evaluation cycles of the students.

Patricia's Story (a Pseudonym)

Patricia taught mathematics to male, adjudicated juveniles in one of the two long-term commitment institutions within the DJJ. While she expressed interest in the concepts of the professional development experience, Patricia approached their implementation in her classroom with a pragmatic perspective. After a group conversation in the first session about the importance of student collaboration to foster higher thinking (Wilhelm, Baker, & Hackett, 2001), Patricia acknowledged, "Whereas this is a wonderful instructional idea, it would require a lot of preparation to implement in a math class with our incarcerated students." The idea of student collaboration in this restrictive environment needed careful consideration. Student behavior was ever present in the minds of the teachers as they planned effective instruction. Patricia learned that teaching students how to collaborate required a commitment of time, patience, and planning.

Patricia was not alone in her assessment of implementing some of the literacy ideas focused on collaborative engagements with students at DJJ. Many teachers, especially those at the commitment institutions, were wary of shifting to a student-centered learning environment, despite our focus throughout the professional development on collaboration and student choice (Jonassen & Land, 2009). As they often reminded us, they taught in environments that included strict protocols to ensure the safety and security of both teachers and students. Once again, we recognized that even though the teachers at DJJ faced challenges due to their environment and student population, they willingly puzzled out and problem solved ways to implement these new ideas, knowing they benefited students.

Kristi's Story (a Pseudonym)

Kristi taught English language arts to female juveniles at an evaluation center. A typical class for Kristi was composed of twelve to fifteen students spanning grades six to twelve. It was not uncommon for teachers to face students who were at different ages, grades, and levels of learning. As a result, differentiating instruction was one of the many challenges teachers faced, and our first session addressed this important issue.

A typical daily lesson in Kristi's class would begin with twenty-five minutes of whole-group reading time where all students read the same novel with teacher guidance. After exploring the concept of balanced literacy (Allison, 2009) in the first session, Kristi shared her new understanding of smaller guided reading groups. She wrote, "My students would most likely feel more confident to share their thinking when interacting with only a few others in the classroom." She further explained, "My students tend to be shy when it comes to reading or sharing out loud in large groups. This is a wonderful lesson, and I plan to use it in my classes."

In the first session, we also shared a best-practice video on connecting reading and writing. Kristi took what she liked from the video and adapted it to meet the learning needs of her female students. First, she had the girls practice with body language as a form of nonverbal communication. Next, she had them take what they understood about the differences between formal and informal tone and apply it to written communication using text messages and e-mails. Kristi noted how this learning engagement helped her students connect what they were learning in school with life. She noted how her students would often address others in an informal tone, and this occasionally escalated to behavioral concerns or issues, especially with adults. In a written reflection, Kristi wrote, "This lesson helped my students understand the need for appropriateness and sensitivity when communicating with others. It also taught my students the importance of considering purpose and audience when writing and speaking as a way to make communicating more comfortable and engaging."

Kristi's story led us to believe that she saw the professional development experience as a way to learn more instructional ideas for impacting not only her students' academic lives but also their social lives. In this way, the professional development had the potential to extend far beyond the classrooms housed behind the fence.

Learning from Their Stories

As we worked alongside the DJJ teachers in the professional development sessions, we shared with them our understanding of instructional literacy ideas, and they shared with us their understanding of teaching adjudicated juveniles. The stories of their successes and challenges provided us with glimpses into their teaching environments; our stories of collaboration and choice provided them with glimpses into what might be possible for their students. We were ever mindful of "taking teachers where they are and gently journeying them to other places" (Robb, 2000, p. 1). We encouraged them to take small steps, remain open to possibilities for providing learning opportunities for the students, and to celebrate learning along the way. We learned how determined they were to be teachers who were learners, growing in their understanding of what it means to be current in the field and effective in the classroom so they could make a difference in the lives of their students.

NEXT STEPS

Throughout our time with the teachers at DJJ, we continuously asked for feedback about ideas they felt they needed more help with in order to strengthen the teaching and learning in their classrooms. From this information, we were able to identify viable ideas for future professional development sessions at DJJ. These ideas included, but were not limited to the following:

• Because motivation is a challenge for our students, we need to learn how to find materials and resources to pique their interests.
• Because many of our students struggle with reading, we need to learn how to help them.
• Because many of our students are challenged with social skills, we need to know more ways to implement collaborative engagements.

• Because our students vary in levels of ability, we need to explore ways to differentiate our instruction to meet the needs of every student.

As we plan our future work with the teachers at DJJ, we are reminded of Aizer and Doyle's (2015) study of the impact of incarceration on a youth's life chances. Findings from their study report that juvenile incarceration decreased the chances of high school graduation by 13 to 39 percentage points and increased the chances of incarceration as an adult by 23 to 41 percentage points, as compared to the average public school student in the same area. Our hope is that by helping the DJJ teachers strengthen and deepen their knowledge of effective literacy instruction, this will make a difference in the educational lives of their adjudicated juvenile students.

REFERENCES

Aizer, A., & Doyle, J. J., Jr. (2015). Juvenile incarceration, human capital, and future crime: Evidence from randomly assigned judges. *The Quarterly Journal of Economics, 130(2),* 759–803.

Allison, N. (2009). *Middle school readers: Helping them read widely, helping them read well.* Portsmouth, NH: Heinemann.

Bourdieu, P. (1986). The forms of capital. In J. Richardson (Ed.), *Handbook of theory and research for the sociology of education* (pp. 241–258). New York, NY: Greenwood Press.

Brozo, W. (2002). *To be a boy, to be a reader: Engaging teen and preteen boys in active literacy.* Newark, DE: International Reading Association.

Daniels, H. (2011). *Comprehension going forward.* Portsmouth, NH: Heinemann.

Gallagher, K. (2004). *Deeper reading: Comprehending challenging texts, 4–12.* Portland, ME: Stenhouse.

Hakim, J. (2007). *Teaching guide for the first Americans: Prehistory–1600.* New York, NY: Oxford University Press.

Herz, S., & Gallo, D. (1996). *From Hinton to Hamlet: Building bridges between young adult literature and the classics.* Westport, CT: Greenwood Press.

Jonassen, D. H., & Land, S. M. (Eds.). (2009). *Theoretical foundations of learning environments.* New York, NY: Routledge.

Nieto, S., & Bode, P. (2012). *Affirming diversity: The sociopolitical context of multicultural education* (6th ed.). Boston, MA: Pearson.

Noddings, N. (2005). *The challenge to care in schools: An alternative approach to education* (2nd ed.). New York, NY: Teachers College Press.

Robb, L. (2000). *Redefining staff development: A collaborative model for teachers and administrators.* Portsmouth, NH: Heinemann.

South Carolina Department of Juvenile Justice. (2016). Retrieved from http://www.state.sc.us/djj/

Wexler, J., Pyle, N., Flower, A., Williams, J., & Cole, H. (2014). A synthesis of academic intervention for incarcerated adolescents. *Review of Educational Research, 84*(1), 3–46.

Wilhelm, J., Baker, T. N., & Hackett, J. D. (2001). *Strategic reading: Guiding students to lifelong literacy 6–12.* Portsmouth, NH: Heinemann.

Index

About the Editors and Contributors

Mary E. Styslinger is an associate professor of English and literacy education at the University of South Carolina, where she directs the Midlands Writing Project. Prior to coming to USC, she was a high school English and theater teacher for twelve years. Her research interests include interweaving literacy into the English curriculum and serving marginalized and at-risk youth; she has published articles in *English Journal*, *Voices from the Middle*, *Language Arts*, *Journal of Adolescent & Adult Literacy*, and *Kappan*.

Karen Gavigan is an associate professor in the School of Library and Information Science at the University of South Carolina. She was a school librarian for fifteen years, and later served as the director of the Teaching Resources Center at the University of North Carolina at Greensboro. Karen and Mindy Tomasevich are coauthors of the book *Connecting Comics to Curriculum: Strategies for Grades 6–12*. Along with Kendra Albright, Karen is coeditor of the graphic novel *AIDS in the End Zone*, which was written by incarcerated youth.

Kendra Albright is professor and director of the School of Library and Information Science at Kent State University and editor of *Libri, International Journal of Libraries and Information Studies*. Dr. Albright's interdisciplinary research addresses issues of information ethics and social justice for minority and disenfranchised populations.

* * *

Deborah Appleman is the Hollis L. Caswell Professor of Educational Studies at Carleton College. Her recent research has focused on teaching college-level language and literature courses at the Minnesota Correctional Facility, Stillwater, for inmates who are pursuing postsecondary education. She is the author and coauthor of several books about literacy learning and teaching, including *Critical Encounters in High School English: Teaching Literary Theory to Adolescents*, *Reading for Themselves: How to Transform Adolescents into Lifelong Readers through Out-of-Class Book Clubs*, *Teaching Literature to Adolescents*, *Adolescent Literacy and the Teaching of Reading*, and *Uncommon Core: Where the Authors of the Standards Go Wrong about Instruction and How You Can Get It Right*, and an edited anthology of her incarcerated students' work, *From the Inside Out: Letters to Young Men and Other Writings: Poetry and Prose from Prison*.

Elizabeth McCall Bemiss received her PhD in language and literacy and a graduate certificate in qualitative research from the University of South Carolina in 2016. She began her career teaching elementary school in an urban district in North Carolina for eight years, during which she received National Board certification in early and middle childhood reading and language arts. She is an assistant professor at the University of West Florida, where she teaches literacy methods courses in the Department of Teacher Education and Educational Leadership. Her research interests concern the intersections between discourses and identity performances, the nature of teacher identity construction, and early and adolescent literacy practices with marginalized youth. Some of her recent research focused on book clubs with incarcerated youth to better understand reader positioning and implications for educators.

Timothy R. Bunch is the district program developer for the South Carolina Department of Juvenile Justice School District, where he taught English and social studies for more than twenty-two years, serving as the program manager and lead teacher of the Communities in Schools (CIS) program, recognized by the National Coalition for Juvenile Justice as one of the top three education and rehabilitation programs in the United States (2001). He was appointed by *USA Today* to the 2004–2005 All-USA Teacher Team, recognizing him as one of the top twenty teachers in the United States (2004), and was honored with the "Best in the Business" Award by the American Correctional Association (2008). He holds a master of education in secondary English and a certificate of graduate study in teaching English to speakers of other languages from the University of South Carolina.

Jennifer L. Doyle is a doctoral candidate in the Department of Curriculum Studies at the University of South Carolina. Informed by her experiences as a former high school English teacher, her primary research interests include promoting equity and social justice in both our educational and criminal justice systems while exploring ways to interrupt the school-to-prison pipeline through the classroom practices of students and teachers. She currently teaches courses in the Department of Instruction and Teacher Education at USC.

Dr. Janie R. Goodman has forty-two years' experience as a language arts educator. In her middle-level classroom, she helped young adolescents grow as lifelong readers and writers. Currently, Janie is a clinical assistant professor in language and literacy/middle-level education at the University of South Carolina, where she teaches undergraduate and graduate courses in content area/disciplinary literacy, English language arts (ELA) methodology, and ELA assessment. Janie has authored several reviews and articles in state and national journals along with continuing to share her expertise in language and literacy through her work with both preservice and practicing classroom teachers.

Vanessa Irvin is an assistant professor of library and information science at the University of Hawaii, Manoa. Dr. Irvin is the author of the award-winning *Readers' Advisory Guide to Street Literature*. Her research interests include reference services, youth services, library services to diverse populations, and librarian professional development.

Susan McNair is in her third year as the librarian at Birchwood School, which serves the South Carolina Department of Juvenile Justice. Since Birchwood is a small school, she performs many duties other than librarian, including textbook coordinator, AdvancED Review chair, data team leader, MAP testing co-coordinator, and member of the leadership team. Previously, she was an elementary librarian for five years and a high school librarian for thirteen years. She reviews materials for and has contributed an article to *School Library Connection*. She is National Board certified and holds specialist and master's degrees in library and information science from the University of South Carolina, as well as a BA in English from Presbyterian College in Clinton, South Carolina.

Megan Mercurio is an English teacher who is National Board certified and has been teaching at the Woodside Learning Center for ten years. While completing her credential at San Francisco State University, Megan started volunteering as a meditation teacher at the San Francisco County Jail, which led to accepting her first full-time teaching job at Woodside Learning Center. Megan lives with her loving husband and young daughter and loves raising her family in San Francisco.

Victoria A. Oglan taught high school English in Canada for thirty-one years, retired, and continued her career at the University of South Carolina as a clinical assistant professor in English and literacy education. She teaches graduate classes in secondary English methodology, teacher research, content literacy, and assessment, and conducts workshops and presentations on a variety of topics related to K–12 education. Her areas of research interest include adolescent literacy, content/disciplinary literacy, high school reading/writing workshop, classroom assessment, and professional development for educators.

Kristine E. Pytash is an associate professor in teaching, learning, and curriculum studies at Kent State University's College of Education, Health, and Human Services, where she codirects the secondary Integrated Language Arts teacher preparation program. Her research focuses on the literacy practices of youth in juvenile detention facilities, disciplinary writing, and preparing teachers to teach writing. In addition, she facilitates a weekly writing workshop for youth at a juvenile detention facility.

Constance Walker is a National Board–certified teacher of exceptional needs. She completed her sociology degree at the University of Connecticut at Storrs. After completing her teaching credential at San Francisco State University, she was recruited to work at Woodside Learning Center as a special education teacher for students with emotional and learning disabilities. She has been teaching at Woodside for eighteen years, and has been team teaching with Megan Mercurio for eight years. She loves watching students demonstrate their abilities and wisdom and lives to see students' joy as they master skills and share their amazing work.

Peter Williamson is an associate professor teaching at Stanford University, where he serves as the faculty director of the Stanford Teacher Education Program for Secondary Teachers. Before coming to Stanford, Peter was an associate professor at the University of San Francisco, where he cofounded the San Francisco Teacher Residency program. Peter earned his doctorate at Stanford, and his interests include urban education, English education, curriculum, and literacy. Peter began his career as a special education teacher working with students who were identified with emotional and behavioral challenges, and then later taught middle and high school English and journalism in the Bay Area's urban schools.